Eliane Karsaklian Ph.D. is an unusual combination of big-picture thinker, academic, and practical businessperson. She has lived and worked in a number of countries, giving her extensive knowledge and experience in negotiation techniques and intercultural relationships. As an internationally known speaker and award-winning researcher, Dr. Karsaklian is currently a visiting professor at the University of Illinois at Chicago. Her most recent book, *The Negotiation Process: Before, During, and After You Close a Deal*, introduces a completely new perspective on international negotiation, providing practical and field-tested examples and guidance to enable readers to implement sustainable negotiation in the real world.

I dedicate this book to all businesspeople enduring stressful and complex negotiation situations. Be ready for a new stressless and enjoyable negotiation world!

Eliane Karsaklian

THE NEGOTIATION PROCESS

Before, During, and After
You Close a Deal

AUSTIN MACAULEY PUBLISHERS™
LONDON • CAMBRIDGE • NEW YORK • SHARJAH

Ordering Information
Quantity sales: Special discounts are available on quantity purchases by corporations, associations, and others. For details, contact the publisher at the address below.

Publisher's Cataloging-in-Publication data
Karsaklian, Eliane
The Negotiation Process

ISBN 9781645752769 (Paperback)
ISBN 9781645752776 (Hardback)
ISBN 9781645752783 (ePub e-book)

Library of Congress Control Number: 2020909136

www.austinmacauley.com/us

First Published (2020)
Austin Macauley Publishers LLC
40 Wall Street, 28th Floor
New York, NY 10005
USA

mail-usa@austinmacauley.com
+1 (646) 5125767

Contents

Introduction:
Anything New Is Disruptive

Did the title of this book surprise you? Probably. This is because for decades we've been taught that negotiation is an act rather than a process and that the negotiation is over once a deal is signed.

But guess what? This is not true. This is a false assumption. But we've been believing it for a while and because of that, we've got in a routine that prevents us from questioning well-settled beliefs. We are not really designed to get out of routine.

Think about how much time you spare to prepare your negotiations. Did you ever design a negotiation strategy? Have you ever brought a negotiation team together to discuss your negotiation strategy in all its details? Did you speak about other factors than price? Did you ever get your negotiation ready on a plane just before landing? Did you ever integrate a cultural analysis into your negotiation strategy?

Now think about how many negotiations you failed. Is there any correlation with the above?

Most people don't spend the needed time to prepare their negotiations. Most people don't think that there are negotiation strategies to design. Most people think that negotiation is all about price. And everyone thinks that the negotiation is over when a deal is signed–at least, in the western world.

But if you are reading this book, it is because you don't want to be like most people. You want to be a successful international negotiator.

The first thing to know is that the only reason you're negotiating with someone is because you need them for something you don't own. You want them to provide you with what you need as much as they want you to provide them with what they need from you. There is no opposition; there is completeness. That means that this is not a competition; you want to collaborate with someone you need for whatever reason it might be.

The second thing to know is that negotiation is not competition; you need what the other negotiator has, and vice versa. Why would you want to be 'against' them? Everyone is interdependent. Instead of winning and losing, what you're actually seeking is sustainable balance and harmony.

The goal of negotiation goes far beyond deals and relationship building. It has to do with sustainability. It has to do with the assurance you should have that the people you negotiate with will keep providing you with what you need, in a way that is not detrimental to anyone.

In this book, I will tell you why people fail their negotiations. Most people think that it has to do with luck – "Sometimes we win. Sometimes we lose." Wrong! First of all, all people involved in a negotiation are responsible for the negotiation outcome. It is not a matter of luck. This kind of assumption only serves people who don't want to be accountable. Second, negotiation is not about winning or losing. Negotiation is about solving problems, finding the resources you need, and thinking about the future of your career and your company.

All these assumptions lead to poor performances because they are easily excused. And because poor performances are ignored, they become the norm. Then, lack of rigor becomes the norm. And this takes us on a high-speed track heading to inaccuracy and mediocrity.

As much as we enjoy having technology to make our lives easier, technology is taking us away from thinking. Movies and TV shows are pure entertainment. They don't require information processing. Home devices are there to do your job for you – they turn on and turn off lights and music, automatically order the products missing in your fridge, and control the garage door…This is very handy, but it prevents you from thinking. The information you get on internet is just copied and pasted on reports. Reviews about products, hotels, and restaurants give you the needed stars for you to pick them without searching for further information and processing it. Your phone reminds you of your meetings so that you don't need to remember them. It does the same with phone numbers and email addresses. And all the apps you have on your phone are made for you to get what you need or want without leaving your couch, not mentioning that now you have a driverless car and you don't need to think about your route.

The first scientists had no tools and their knowledge was based on observation, calculations (without computers), deep thinking, and interactions with the real world. And most of them got it right. Sophisticated thinking is more powerful than sophisticated machinery. Einstein's lab was his fountain pen. The pyramids are still standing in Egypt, while several modern bridges have been falling apart and killing hundreds of people. Such disasters are not caused by lack of technology or sophisticated tools. They are caused by lack of rigor and analytical thinking.

Don't get me wrong. I am not at all against technology. But I am against replacing interactions between humans and conversations in the real world and thinking. I am against shallow beliefs and the illusion of knowing without really knowing. The consequences we will experience in few years because of shallow behaviors, lack of critical thinking, and rigor will be dramatic. That is why you should invest in people and relationships as much or more than you invest in equipment.

Control Your Own Destiny or Someone Else Will

The first step in succeeding a negotiation is having a clear idea of what you want to obtain from the negotiation. Think clearly about what you want and why you want it. You need to personally and genuinely want it and not just do what someone else told you to do. Think about how pertinent and realistic your request is – are you really in a position to obtain what you want?

Is it about getting what you want and need or is it about winning over someone else? Keep in mind that winning implies competition, not negotiation. Winning and fighting are the opposites of negotiation. If you focus on winning, you lose sight of your real needs and goals. In other words, if your goal is to win, you should not be involved in a negotiation.

Most negotiators don't see their partners (or counterparts as they are awfully called) as people they want to be in a relationship with for long. They negotiate a deal for the short term. Then, they switch to other partners and many others again, searching for the lowest price, or the trendy novelty, or a brand name as an endorsement. Nothing sustainable. Nothing deep. At the end, these companies are known as opportunistic and unreliable. They are seen as unstable people with whom one cannot envisage any future.

This is not what you want to be. You don't want to be the one who competes, closes the 'best' deals for your company, and leaves all the consequent issues to pervade your relationships in such a way that you should always be in search for other options. Have you ever thought about the costs of searching for new partners all the time? What you save in getting the lowest price at some deals, you spend in recruiting new partners later on.

If you think short term, short term is all you'll get. Don't expect to get sustainable results from short-term deals. Rather, you need to think about the future–your future and the future of your company which won't be what you want it to be alone. If you want your company to be around for long, you need to aim at sustainable growth.

In international business, no company can reach sustainable growth alone. You need to get the right partners for that. Get married to the right people. Couple with people who can help you to go the distance. You need them and they need you for their own growth.

They might be far away. They might be in countries you've never been before, speak a different language, and have different habits. You need to learn how to talk with them. You need to see your future together across countries, cultures, and markets. You need to open up to sustainability with no boundaries.

If you want to be successful, you need to have your goals very clear. If you are unclear, you'll be lost in the midst of average companies. Remember that a contract is just theory on a piece of paper. Reality hits when you enforce the contract. Focus on your goals with magnifying lenses. When things get tough, your purpose for the future will keep you focused and push you to overcome adversity. Your energy comes from your purpose and makes you grow.

Cultural Differences Are a Blessing

Culture has become both a practice and an issue in international business. It is a practice because, well, business is practiced internationally today, and it is an issue because all that is said about working across cultures seems to be problematic. Some people are making money by just telling others how to work with the Chinese, or the Indians, or with any other 'mysterious' cultures in the world in one single training day–as if we could learn about other cultures in one day!

But we certainly forgot that international business is nothing new. In the old times, we had already interacted across cultures and learned and inherited from one another. We learned about the stars with the Babylonians, have paper to write on, thanks to the Chinese, and count with numbers created by the Indians.

The Chinese had already understood magnetism and created the compass while practicing the traditional Chinese medicine based on herbs which are now used in the western world. Egyptians had advanced surgical tools, enabling them to extract the main body organs from pharaohs before mummifying them. Indians practiced eye surgery in eliminating cataract. And the most famous atomist was Democritus in Greece.

The first international negotiators in the world were the Phoenicians, sailing back and forth around the Mediterranean Sea, buying and selling products from all countries. India and China were part of a vast overland and overseas trading networks channeled along the spice routes. And their people had developed writing and science to a high level. Science benefited trade, and the wealth from trade allowed to study. So, science and international negotiation have been interconnected ever since.

Science is the best way of finding out about the world and everything in it, which includes us. For most of human history, science has been used alongside magic, religion, and technology to try to understand and control the world. Today, we aim at separating science from all 'irrational' practices. What was compatible before is made incompatible now. First, Descartes asserted that body and soul were two separate and disconnected things. Then there were theories about intelligence quotient, more often called IQ, which aimed at measuring (rationally) peoples' ability to think and analyze. Then it was discovered that humans have more than one type of intelligence and new theories came up. Today, we talk about emotional intelligence which is the ability to identify others' emotions and respond accordingly, and cultural intelligence (CQ) is the ability of knowing and understanding other cultures and behaving accordingly. Now, rational and irrational are mixed.

Be a Motion Machine

The main goal of this book and the parallel with science is to help international negotiators to broaden their visions of intercultural interactions and of the negotiation process itself. It is an invitation to leave behind the old certainties and to venture in what is needed to be a successful sustainable negotiator in international settings today. It has as much to do with saving the planet as with saving businesses.

As you read through the pages, I hope you will be inspired to apply these ideas. Through understanding the international negotiation process differently, you will improve your business drivers, experience less stressful situations, get to more fruitful interactions, and engage in more profitable endeavors.

While reading these pages, you might think that this does not apply to you, who is comfortable with the widespread negotiation theories. But if you do apply them, you'll be among those who understood that the business landscape has changed since the 1970s and 1980s and that sustainability is not just a term we use but a real business driver at all levels of businesses. And you will experience the delights of working in a more pleasant and stress-free way.

When people think of science, they tend to think about labs, test tubes, microscopes, and molecules. They tend to see it from very far away and don't think their business might have something to do with it. Mainly when people are in sales force, procurement, or marketing departments, they think that science is all about another world. But physics is the science that studies nature, and all humans are part of nature and we interact with it as much as we interact with other humans. Science happens all around us each and every day.

Thinking and acting towards sustainability is not a trend or even less an option; it is a need and an obligation. Climate change is one of the most pressing global concerns of the twenty-first century. Glaciers are retreating and subtropical deserts are expanding. Extreme weather events such as droughts and heavy snowfalls are more frequent, species of plants and animals are vanishing, and food security is threatened. While the northern countries are freezing, southern countries are melting with extremely high temperatures, which require the use of more energy. Energy use lies at the core of these global warming trends. As the world economy grows, people are using more and more energy.

Now think about your business. With all these mergers and acquisitions happening every year, are your options increasing or decreasing? In merged markets, do you have more or less companies to work with? Well, just like the planet, your resources are becoming scarce too. You will spend much more energy in looking for other options every time you fail your negotiations.

Now you need to look for other options because, for some reason, you no longer want to work with your former partners, or they don't want to work with you anymore. You might think that there are several options on the market and perhaps plenty of partners can bring you the resources you need to propel growth. But which are the ones you want to hang out with in the future? And how many options are left to you now that others are already engaged in sustainable relationships? How much energy will you need to deploy in order to find the people you want to build a future with?

The belief that globalization is expanding the markets is a myth. You might work across borders, but the companies you work with are part of big international corporations. They are no longer independent entities. In reality, markets are shrinking. This is the right time to pick the partners you want to work with in a lasting relationship. The more you wait, the lesser the options there will be left for you.

Look for companies you have things to share with: values, a vision of future, perspectives, and innovative thinking. Look for them around the world. Then learn about their culture to facilitate your interactions. Design your growth strategy together. Use strengths from all parties to leverage your growth and beat your competitors. Think about collaboration rather than confrontation. And know the others' cultures. Be sensitive to their distinctive characteristics so as not only to unintentionally offend but also to be true to your own cultural standards. Allow all parties to learn from one another.

The Way You Go About Your Life Tells About Your Values

If you take negotiation as a battle you should survive and win, your behavior will be aggressive, and aggressiveness is all you will get back from others. Moreover, your focus will be on beating others rather than being creative and objective in the search for the best sustainable deal. You will not even think about collaboration.

History shows us how much war can change behaviors. Researchers' job is to collaborate so that we can get to more comprehensive findings and progress. However, when the nuclear bomb was created, researchers stopped publishing and collaborating with colleagues and it all turned into secrecy and competition. You don't want this to happen to your business.

Getting into sustainable negotiation is an inside-out process. It is about consciousness and mindset. As soon as you understand the benefits of sustainable negotiation, you will regret having wasted so much time, energy, and effort in using the old practices in negotiation. Sustainable negotiation will take you and your company to higher levels of progress and performance. The mind shift needed for you to give way to sustainable negotiation will require less effort and energy than all the failures you might have already experienced in past negotiations.

Never ever again will you go to a negotiation fearing the outcomes, armed up to your teeth to defend yourself from the people you need. You will get rid of the pressure of winning. You will take your time to select your partners, to converse with them, to get to know them, and to design your growth together.

This book is organized in three main parts, each one representing one phase of the negotiation process – before, during, and after a deal is closed.

The first part (Part I) will explain all the steps you need to go through when preparing your negotiation, which is a fundamental step in succeeding your negotiations. Lack of preparation leads to lack of information and less confidence during the negotiation. You can be surprised by situations that were predictable if you had better prepared and thus visualized your negotiation. Negotiation is a strategic process. You need to design your negotiating strategy prior to meeting the people you will negotiate with.

Part II will show you how to behave during the negotiations. Knowing how to get along with your potential partners is crucial in succeeding your negotiation. Your team's professional and social behaviors determine the kind of relationship you can establish with other companies.

Part III will tell you how to sustain your relationship with your partners. Your life together starts when you agree to work together, that is, when you sign a deal. Most companies fall into the pitfall of well-behaving until the signature of a contract and then totally neglect their interactions and follow-ups with the people they were committed to work with. The after-deal is as important as any other stage of the negotiation process for the relationships to be sustainable.

Part I
Before the Negotiation

"Failing to prepare is preparing to failing."
Franklin

Part I
Before the Beginning

*Not finding evidence of something doesn't mean it
didn't occur.*

Chapter 1: International Negotiation and Physics – Two Parallel Worlds

After spending most of my career in international negotiation, I've noticed there's a parallel here. Businesspeople have been taught to view negotiation as a competition. This is akin to the classical physics approach of determinism. If you look at the groups involved in a negotiation and the resources at their disposal, you can determine which will be the winners and which the losers.

Newton stated that an object will stay at rest or continue moving toward the ground at the same speed unless it encounters an outside force. The same thing happens when you are negotiating. You can keep going with your strategy, ideas, and propositions until they hit someone's objections. Then your offers either change their trajectories to adjust to the objections or stop as if they had hit a wall. Just as with energy, your propositions are not created or destroyed during a negotiation; they are transformed.

But I believe negotiation has moved beyond this model, with its roots in the western world. Increasing numbers of businesspeople are coming from the Asian, the Middle-Eastern, and South American cultures. Their viewpoints are different. They operate more often with the quantum physics approach of probabilities. This means they can hold what appears to be opposing viewpoints at the same time.

That is why they look unpredictable to most westerners. Their thinking patterns and their behaviors are not linear and can surprise others by bending around obstacles until they reach their goals. There is no clear-cut position in these cultures as opposed to the American culture, for instance. It is a waste of time to try to determine their trajectory. We can only talk about probabilities of future behaviors.

If American and Western-European businesspeople want to remain relevant in the global marketplace, they need to move beyond the classical model of negotiation.

Indeed, contemporary ideas about negotiation can be traced back to 1981. This is when members of the Harvard Negotiation Project wrote *Getting to Yes: Negotiating Agreement Without Giving In*. This book is one of the longest running business paperback bestsellers. They applied a deterministic approach to negotiation. If you knew the exact position of your partners and how their minds worked, you could predict their future behavior and would have no surprises when negotiating with them. The outcome of your negotiation would only depend on the consistency of your own strategy and the way you manage the information you have about your partners.

Their book also incorporated some negotiating strategy ideas from game theory that are still accepted today: win-win and win-lose.

Win-win strategy has become the norm because it's politically correct. A negotiator's goal is to arrive at beneficial outcomes for all parties. Negotiators search for collaboration and are more likely to make concessions and avoid conflicts. It also means that you want to create good relationships with the other side, even if you don't get as much as you could out of that specific business. The strategy has a long-term orientation.

Win-win tries to be an integrative approach. Objectives, constraints, and the needs of all parties are factored into the process. It also means that one party's problems become *all* parties' problems, to which a common solution should be found. Working together to find solutions to all of these issues means the global gains are bigger and shared by everybody. Negotiators believe that the process and outcomes must be fair for both sides— for the length of the agreement.

Win-lose strategy is used when negotiators don't believe all parties can win. Their aim becomes protecting their own interests. The rationale is that other people's problems are *not* their problems. In this approach, people aren't interested in being transparent and sharing gains. However, the result doesn't always look aggressive and can be very subtle. In addition, negotiators may announce win-win intentions but get into a win-lose strategy as the talks progress.

Another possibility is that the negotiation starts with a win-win or a win-lose strategy and turns into a lose-lose one. Several factors can lead to confrontation, so each party says to the other, "If you don't give me what I want, I won't give anything to you." The one who adjusts the most is seen as needing the other more—and losing.

I consider these ideas classical negotiation. My concern is that these—like classical physics—can no longer explain the negotiating universe. Newton's ideas worked fine with the behavior of larger bodies, but other theories and equipment were needed to deal with subatomic particles. We can parallel classical physics with what we can see, and quantum physics with what exists but we can't see.

Here is the parallel with people. We can see what they do through their behavior, but we can't see the underlying reasons for their behavior. We need tools that enable us to identify what is influencing their actions. That means understanding attitudes, opinions, motivations, fears, and culture. When you work mainly with people from other cultures, you can only think about probabilities.

Change Is a Chance

People in high positions in companies feel like they have all figured out; otherwise they wouldn't be in such positions. They also think that showing that they can still learn or have hesitations about some topics is a sign of weakness. It is also a matter of pride. The truth is that they are insecure and fearful people. And what if they were wrong? Well, they are already wrong because they are narrow-minded and refuse to see beyond the commonplace. If we settle for the obvious, we'll never see what's beyond it.

Reluctance to change is caused by social pressure and the status quo created around what is obvious and shallow to rule out those who see further than the average person. Is it because they are more intelligent? Not necessarily, but it is certainly because they are curious and dare contesting the well-settled mediocre standards to look out for better options. Curiosity lies at the heart of science.

Aristotle, to whom the loss of curiosity equaled death, stated, "All men by nature desire to know." Aristotle spent his whole life learning and teaching. As a natural philosopher and a lover of wisdom, he focused on logic – how we can think more clearly.

Indeed, there is a risk of being discriminated and excluded from the mainstream system when thinking differently. This happened to Galileo, Copernicus, and so many other thinkers and scientists, thanks to whom we learned and are less ignorant today. But in their time, they were persecuted, although what they discovered was accurate. Luckier than Copernicus, Galileo was helped by the use of scientific method. We would think that showing evidence through empirical observation and mathematical demonstration was harder to contest. And yet, it was contested. The same thing happens in companies and societies today. You'd better fit in or you're out.

Trust, innovation, and inspiration are values written in all companies' charts, but reality is that you are welcome if you comply with the status quo instead of suggesting something too different. Something that requires effort and reviewing what has been done for decades is not welcome, even if the current results are not satisfactory.

You can also blame others for what happens to you, but you need to take responsibility because what happens to you is the result of what you think and what you do. Remember that all scientific discoveries and revelations came from curiosity and from asking questions about what we could see and what we couldn't see. You have the power of changing the direction of your life and of your company. You do that by asking yourself the right questions. It is not because we all use technology that we have an innovative mindset. We use it because it provides us comfort.

If we had all figured out and if asking new questions was not a real need, researchers and scientists would be unemployed. Their job is precisely to ask questions and to challenge what we think we already know. Isaac Newton thought he had it all figured out. Two centuries later, modern physicists showed that there was much more in nature than what Newton could see. And today, scientists know that what we don't know far exceeds what we know.

Other than lack of curiosity, it is intriguing that people wouldn't feel that excitement of not knowing. Every new discovery is exciting. Every new concept, idea, and experience should get people excited and wanting to know more. *What*, *why*, and *how* are good questions but 'because this is the way it is,' conformity is a bad answer.

In the seventeenth century, the French Philosopher and Mathematician René Descartes stated that body and mind were two separate and unrelated things: "There is nothing in the concept of body that belongs to the mind and nothing in that of the mind that belongs to the body." Descartes rejected the idea that spirit and science could co-exist, although he believed that both mind and matter were created by God. To him, the human body was a machine and the human brain was the center of intelligence and reason.

By that time, it was believed that the universe and people were made of physical matters until scientists from the twentieth century started to dig deeper on the matters of universe and discovered that there were more than physical matters in the universe. But Galileo had already suggested that universe is not all material. *Au contraire*, it is essentially non-physical. We know today that the universe arises from a field that is even more subtle than energy, a field that looks more like information, intelligence, or consciousness than matter.

Greek Philosopher Democritus said, "Nothing exists but atoms and empty space. Everything else is opinion." This might come as a brutal statement but it leads to possible interpretations. Some will say that opinions are not real and accurate, so let's just stick with the atoms while others could be interested in what opinions would say about these atoms and the empty space in order to have a better understanding of them.

In the eighteenth century, German Philosopher Emmanuel Kant pointed out that human beings can never truly know the nature of reality as it is. Our investigations only provide answers to the questions we ask, which are based on the capabilities and limitations of our minds. Our perception of the world is fundamentally dependent on the filters of our consciousness.

This makes me think of a company I worked with right after they went through a big crisis. Their chairman had made discriminatory statements during an interview with a journalist and his company suffered from boycotts, bad brand reputation, and loss of market share in several countries. Then, I had the opportunity of meeting some of the people who worked in key positions in the company. During our interviews, I made it clear that I would write a case study based on their story. They all told me how much effort their leaders had made to recover from the crisis and how genuinely non-exclusionary their intentions and actions were.

Then I wrote the case study citing their own words, which I had recorded during the interviews and showed to them prior to publication. They wanted to change everything. The mirror-effect made them realize that although all they had told me was very positive towards their leaders, they were not allowed to speak on behalf of the company. They also realized, without saying it, that the story was too perfect to be credible by others. In other words, they couldn't believe their own words at such a point that they questioned what they knew I had recorded. They had created their own reality during the interviews.

This is how much of a filter perception can be. When seen from the inside, their role was to protect their company and leadership by telling and showing how perfect the company had learned to be as a consequence of the crisis. But when the same story was reflected back to them, they had an external vision of it which was inconsistent with their consciousness.

Perception is what makes us think what reality is like. But we don't have the same perception of the same things. These differences have to do with imagination, background, curiosity, and so forth. And because not everything can be measured, perception has more to do with creating reality than putting up with it.

Don't Live on Illusions

We need to drop the concept that any side 'wins.' Negotiation isn't a win-lose boxing match in which one party is the victor and the other leaves the arena in an ambulance. What incentive does the 'defeated' group have in continuing to work with the winner? Frankly, they have more reason to do as little as possible, or perhaps even scuttle the agreement later (particularly if a better opportunity comes along).

Although this idea might sound shocking to you, it is imperative that we stop believing in win-win negotiation strategies, because it's an illusion. You can't have two winners. Winning has to do with competition as in games, sports, or fights. Instead, we need to move to *sustainable negotiation*, a term I recently coined. In most parts of the world, you no longer do a deal and then leave. Each side has something the other needs, and they must work together to achieve their goals. To do this, you engage in a collaboration that continues to evolve. This leads to repeated contact, discussions and negotiations, constant adjustments, and perhaps alterations to the original contract. Your goal becomes cooperation and balance.

That means you consider the other negotiator as your 'mirror' or 'twin' rather than your rival. It requires you to stop thinking that person's culture–perhaps of not valuing being on time or wanting to go to a movie in the middle of a negotiation–is different and bad. Instead, you must be open to learning from others about alternatives that never would have occurred to you.

It also involves the challenge of a paradox: something else we're borrowing from quantum mechanics. To achieve sustainable negotiation, you must hold two points of view in your mind at the same time: yours and your negotiating partner's, even if they sound inconsistent. You are being asked to move from the classical negotiation/classical physics approach of determinism– you should pick *either* one option *or* another–to the sustainable negotiation/quantum mechanics approach of probabilities. Two opposing options are not exclusive and you can choose *both* of them if they happen simultaneously.

What you are saying should be unique.

Chapter 2: Words Carry Messages

Lavoisier asserted that to do good science, you need to be precise in the words you use because we think only through the medium of words.

It might look as a detail but if we use words to communicate with others, it is because they convey messages. *Winning* and *losing* have to do with competition, not with collaboration or with partnership. *Counter* means against – counteroffer, counterargument, counterpart, and so forth. And *closing* means end. Closing a deal means the end of the negotiation if we believe that the negotiation stops when a deal is signed, except that it doesn't. It keeps going during all the time you are working with your partners.

It is not because you don't think about the meaning of these words every day that their meaning doesn't remain the same. In sustainable negotiation, we don't talk about closing a deal, counterpart, the people on the other side of the table, and any of these words and expressions that oppose you to the people you want to work with. It is because you want these people on your side, not against you. You need them. They will help you to grow and to beat your competitors. Your competition is with your competitors, not with your partners.

You might be skeptical about sustainable negotiation because it seems too easy, too nice, and too disruptive. You were taught to be a tough negotiator and to get to a deal as fast as possible. I can understand that because the same happens with science and because I was taught the same theories. But I got tired of failing my negotiations and of lacking the knowledge to do better.

Disruptive theories have four stages of acceptance:

1. It is worthless nonsense.
2. This is interesting, but perverse.
3. This is true but quite unimportant.
4. I always said so.

In the history of science, there is enough evidence of how narrow-minded people have behaved across all the stages of scientific discoveries. But there was always someone to go the distance and challenge the deep-rooted beliefs. And thanks to them, we know much more and better about our world today. If you want to be among the successful ones, you need to see negotiation from a totally different perspective. You can be a trendsetter, the one who succeeds negotiations internationally and paves the path to better business outcomes.

Your vision of future will shape the way you conduct business. Future is not a destiny. It is a consequence of what you are doing today. The same applies to destiny. William Jennings Bryanhas already said, "Destiny is not a matter of chance; it is a matter of choice. It is not a thing to be waited for; it is a thing to be achieved."

If you want to achieve sustainable growth, you need to engage into sustainable relationships with your partners, which you will get, thanks to sustainable negotiation.

Share What You Want People to Know

You may say, "This is just a matter of semantics," or "They choose words they think will help sell books." I believe it goes much deeper than this.

Look at the language we use to describe negotiation: adversary, argue your case, brinksmanship, good cop/bad cop, haggling, negotiating against someone, the other side, the opposition, counterparty, and counterargument. When we use terms such as these, it seems we're inviting conflict—even if there wasn't any to begin with. You put the person on the other side— opposed to you, not next to you.

I contest win-win in negotiation, and it is not just a matter of semantics. Words matter more than you would think because they reflect people's thoughts. If you are focused on protecting yourself from others, then you'll never allow them to be on your side—as hard as they may try to show you that they're with you, not against you. They will never get in if you don't open the door to your mind.

Let's get back to competition. It is easy to see how people cheat in sports because the only goal is to win. Athletes are there to win—whatever it takes. There is not a single Olympic game without a doping scandal. Doping is cheating. It's illegal, yet it is done. Why? To enhance the probability of beating other competitors and to win. Although unethical, this approach to competition makes sense, as there is only one gold medal for a game. Athletes are there to compete, not to collaborate. Everyone has forgotten the spirit of Olympics and the savvy words of Baron de Coubertin, "What matters is to compete, not to win."

To my mind, this has nothing to do with negotiation. Sadly, most people think it does. That is a matter of perception.

Perceptual Tricks and Duality

Perception begins when our sensory neurons pick up information from the environment and send it to the brain in the form of electrical impulses. When we work with other people, what we actually see is the perception we have of them based on their physical appearance, tone of voice, language, accent, and behavior, etc., but we think this is how they are in reality and we react to that 'reality.'

There is nothing neutral in this process. If we see something our brain can't identify, we grab onto something similar, something our brain is familiar with, and we say, "It is like…"

If there is nothing close or is something we know not to be real, we just discard it as being a product of our imagination.

As children are allowed to be imaginative, they learn commonsense by bumping into reality. Life doesn't come with an instruction book. But we should learn how to live.

The intuitive laws of biology and physics are learned by interacting with the real world. As adults, we are forced to leave imagination behind and to be rational. This is what we call socialization. But today, children are more and more involved in a dual process, as they live between their games and imagination on the one side and reality coming through their devices on the other side.

Being able to deal with duality is paramount because the universe is governed by two sets of laws. The laws of Newton stated four centuries ago still explain behaviors of matters that are our size and that we can see, while the laws of quantum physics govern everything we can't see but make possible the existence of everything we see, that is, atoms and subatomic particles.

But the universe is not limited to what we see and what we don't see. In the world that we don't see, there are also opposed and similar matters. In the 1930s, physicists realized that for every particle there is a twin − an antiparticle − but with an opposite charge. The first antiparticle to be discovered was the antielectron, called the positron, which has a positive charge. The positron is identical to the electron in every way, except that it carries the opposite charge.

Thus, in a world of similarities and differences, nothing can be absolutely good or bad because all is relative. As an example, opposites were beneficial, as they were practiced by Galen in Greece. As a physician, he would use the opposite remedy to treat illnesses. So, illnesses that are hot and moist should be treated with remedies that are cold and dry and conversely. It is just a matter of balance and compensation. It is also a matter of completeness.

When we negotiate with others, aren't we looking for the missing part of our business? Aren't we looking for completeness through resources we don't have? Aren't we trying to enhance our strengths to be more competitive? So why would we take other parties as enemies? Why would we oppose rather than associate? Your (potential) partners are resources you need to propel growth.

We live in a world of contradictions, but contradictory doesn't mean conflicting. Options might differ but this is not always a bad thing. *Au contraire*, it can be very positive because it pushes you beyond what is obvious. Remember that there is more than one way to deal with a given situation.

Make Sure Your Message Is Getting Across

More often than not, people blame the other parties for unsuccessful outcomes to their business because they don't want to go through all the trouble of questioning what they have done. It is a lack of introspection; it is easier to blame what is outside than to reconsider what comes from the inside. In fact, dualism pervades our lives as does the understanding of it – in there/out there, subject/object, science/spirit, consciousness/reality, and mind/matter. There is no cause/effect in duality; there is only creating a reality together.

Descartes introduced the notion of dualism, stating that the universe was made up of two completely different kinds of things: matter (tangible) and spirit (intangible). This way, the human body is matter and his soul is spirit. What opposed both was that the matter has substance and occupies space while the spirit is the opposite, located nowhere without any material basis at all.

Today, we know that thoughts and behaviors are part of the same thing. If it is personal, we call it an attitude. If it's cultural, we call it a paradigm and if it's universal, we call it a law. We create the effects of reality all the time. Often, when making decisions, it is easier to say that we had no choice than to admit it was our choice to pick that one because it was easier and we didn't want to face the unknown consequences of other choices.

When you work with other people, there is the phenomenon of entanglement. We could also call this interdependence. What you do to an electron happens to its twin even if it is very, very far away. As two electrons are entangled (their wave functions beat in unison), when you measure the spin on one of them (up), you already know that the other one is spinning down even if they are separated by many light-years. Whatever happens to one automatically has an effect on the other.

The same phenomenon happens in our relationships with others. Every action and every word that has an impact on us has an impact on them, perhaps not the same one due to different perceptions and cultural differences. But there is an impact anyway. This is our world of abstract thought. After all, we see what we want to see because we ask ourselves and others questions that give us the answers we want to hear. Perception is a selective mechanism.

The process of observing has an influence on what is observed, and science was forced to drop four centuries of assumptions and realize that we are involved in reality. Reality is a consequence of our thoughts and our actions. We are intrinsic to the whole process of reality because our involvement creates reality. Memory leads to perception, which leads to observation and consequently to reality. We see the reality as we perceive it and this is based on our past experiences. Thus, we rarely share the same reality. This is what is frequently and wrongly defined as culture shock.

It is remarkable that in an era of technological development and with the accumulation of so much knowledge across centuries, businesses are still conducted based on old beliefs. Creativity should not be limited to launching of new products. While companies invest in research and development for the conception of new products, their management and negotiation beliefs remain the same old ones. Culture shock already starts within the companies because of that. Unsuccessful outcomes in business should be seen as facts that must lead to other strategies and practices as a springboard to more appropriate mentalities and actions. Most failures in the market place are due to poor management and lack of preparation in negotiations. But people are even capable to deny such facts, just not to change.

Darwin has said that only the ones who adapt can survive. And he stated this after having observed plants, animals, and bugs. Pasteur and Koch came up with the same findings when studying bacteria. They all adapt to very unknown and harsh environments to survive. Why wouldn't humans do so?

Darwin presented two types of selections – the natural selection in which only the strongest survive and the artificial selection, where people pick the strongest and best traits and multiply them. This is how we have seedless fruits today. In the marketplace, artificial selection is what makes the difference. Being conscious of your strengths and weaknesses, underscoring what you are good at, specializing in what you do better than others, hiring the right people for the right jobs, having a clear positioning, and partnering with the right people leverage your growth.

One fact is that more than three billion dollars are spent in mergers and acquisitions each year and two thirds of them prove to fail. So why do CEOs keep doing it without better preparation and strategic thinking? The unsuccessful outcomes of these operations are facts caused by unprepared people with inappropriate strategies. Yet, CEOs from all over the world will keep recreating the same situations (reality) over and over again, no matter how much money is wasted, how much unemployment their unsuitable strategies are generating, and how much frustration is created at all levels of companies and societies.

People hardly wonder how many possibilities exist before making a decision. As quantum physics is about possibilities, when you always recreate the same reality by always making the same decision with the same limited information, with the same fear of the unknown, you are not only blocking all the ways of evolution for your business but you are also missing the quantum of your life. "Life is not about finding yourself. Life is about creating yourself," Shaw would say. But creating what has already been is hardly creating.

"Fortune favors the prepared minds."
Louis Pasteur

Chapter 3: Preparing Your Negotiation

This quote from Dr. Louis Pasteur was true about his experiments which led to a process for neutralizing the bacteria that soured milk, wine, and beer, as well as vaccinations for anthrax and rabies. Now you know you can embrace the ideas from physics and quantum mechanics as a way to move forward in your career and to lead your company into more successful international negotiations.

It is not easy to be different, to come up with innovative ideas, and to get out of the status quo and do what others would never dare doing. Back in the old days, people who dared seeing what we were not supposed to see were burned as witches and wizards. You shouldn't go counter-flow. This is why most people just go with the flow without giving much thought to what they should be actually doing or of what they are missing. It seems easier to complain about their jobs and wait desperately for the weekend and holidays than to change to a job where they take pleasure to do what they do every day.

This need or obligation of conformity was already questioned by Mark Twain: "If a man doesn't believe as we do, we say he is a crank, and that settles it. I mean, it does nowadays because now we can't burn him."

Some people have a broader vision of situations. For instance, facing the relentless insistence of one side about something they don't really need but want to get it just to win. The other side, more mature, decides to give them what they want so that they stop whining. In doing so, they gave the other side the feeling of victory, but all they did was throw them a bone. This is what happens when people aim at winning. They will even be subjected to this type of humiliation just to think that they won.

Now let's take a moment to think about the consequences of this kind of situations, which unfortunately happens very often. The team which thought they won will realize later that they did not win. Their happiness will be ephemeral and their hangover will be bitter. The side that 'let them win' lost all respect for them and would still be savoring the moment when the other side accepted so joyfully the bone they threw at them.

This prompts the question: how will these people work together after this? They diverge in everything. Their goals are different, their vision of negotiation is different, and there is no mutual respect anymore. This is the perfect example of a non-sustainable situation. Their relationship is going nowhere.

Lying Is Useful

People start by lying to themselves and trying to convince themselves that they have the life they chose. But a lie is a disconnection with reality. A lie is something that is not and yet people tend to believe more in what is not than what is. This is called denial. It prevents you from facing reality, the reality you helped to create. You lie once and people believe you. You are relieved because you didn't need to tell the (ugly?) truth, that is, face reality. Then you lie again, and again, and again. It turns into an easy thing to do, and then it becomes an automatic behavior of yours, so much so that you are the first one believing your lies. You create a parallel life to yourself, the one that is unreal but the one you'd rather believe in because you like it better than your real life. So why don't you just change your life instead of pretending to have a better one?

If you lie in negotiation, you are making your own job harder. When you tell a deliberate lie, you have to be holding in mind the truth because you know the truth. Lying is hard work because in requires more brain activity. When you start lying, you need to keep lying or admit that you lied. The first one will drag you to a spiral of lies that you should remember so that you don't betray yourself during the next conversations. And you do all this while holding the truth in your mind. It requires a lot of energy and information processing. If you admit you have lied, the outcome is unpredictable. You might be praised by recognizing it and asking for forgiveness or blamed for being a liar. Remember that the solid base for business is trust. Lies and trust are incompatible. And thanks to technology, it is easier to check all information online in real time.

Sometimes people get so used to lying that anything different seems to be a lie. Remember the film *Life of Pi*.

This shipwrecked boy from India having survived alone from a sinking ship, where his family was, endures the most amazing adventure in a lifeboat with a tiger. He spends the whole time negotiating with the tiger in order the keep himself alive. When he is finally rescued and taken to a hospital, the staff asks him to tell what happened. Every time he tells the truth, people disbelieve him. At the end, he decides to lie and tell some average story so that it would seem plausible to people and they wouldn't think he had lost his mind with the tragedy.

Get Ready to Negotiate Successfully

Invest (not spend) time in preparing your negotiation. You will be preparing to be successful.

It is always useful to gather opinions from other people while you are preparing your negotiation, mainly from people who have already worked with those you will meet with. But you should at the same time conduct your independent research on the side.

You should also beware of briefings and advices from those who speak on behalf of others. Keep in mind that they are conveying their own perception of others which can be accurate or misleading. Consider the following situation.

Last year, I was asked by a person in Austria to come over and talk to her team about international interactions. I asked for more details about which aspect of international interactions she was interested in – communication, negotiation, marketing… Her answer was pretty evasive, as she wanted 'a little bit of everything.'

I knew that it wouldn't be possible, so I asked for more details, which I didn't get. As I didn't have access to the participants, I decided to start my approach with communicating internationally and then let me be guided by the participants' questions, except that there were no questions.

I could feel during my speech that before lunch, I had already lost the attention and interest of half of the participants. Then, few days later, her feedback on behalf of the participants was that they were expecting me to give them concrete answers, tips, and tools for their specific needs. The only people who were happy with my presentation were those who asked me specific questions about situations they were experiencing and got concrete answers to their issues over lunch. All other participants just stayed there, passively waiting for me to bring solutions to their problems which of course, I was not familiar with.

What happened here? I couldn't prepare my presentation more accurately because of lack of information. At no moment I was informed about their specific needs. On the other side, the middle person had promised her team that they would get all the tools to solve all their intercultural problems. As our respective information and thus expectations didn't match, our outcome was disappointing to both parties. Don't let others lead you to misperformance because for some reason, they don't disclose the information you need to be well prepared.

Luckily, the negotiation process is constituted of several steps and rounds, unlike a one-day gig. When negotiating, you first need to make the difference between what the people you are negotiating with want and what they need. People want many things but these are not always what they need. People tend to want what is easier and avoid what they need. They would rather have you lying to them than confronting them in order to help them with what they need.

One year ago, a very good friend of mine died of cancer. He had been diagnosed two years before and the cancer was progressing very quickly. He was trying to fight his disease but was not doing enough. All people around him would all the time encourage him to keep doing what he was already doing, telling him that he was doing great while he looked more and more like a zombie. I was the only one confronting him and explaining to him that if he didn't have the right lifestyle, the treatment alone wouldn't make any miracle. He was upset because I was negative, while everybody else was kind to him. Indeed, everyone else was very kind to him, but no one tried to help him at any level. He ended up living a miserable life until he died. People would tell him what he wanted to hear, not what he needed to hear. This is a good example of the expression: "Silence kills."

Step-by-Step Preparation

Start your preparation by conducting an extensive market analysis. Understand your market and their market. The last thing you want to happen is to be informed about existing information from the people you will work with. This will be even worse if it is about your own market. Be ready to converse about any topic linked to both markets. Most importantly, allocate the needed time to get ready to your negotiation. Start with a market analysis.

Market Analysis

Use tools to analyze the markets. The PESTLE analysis will help you to understand the macro-environment in terms of political, economic, social, technological, legal, and environmental factors. Then the Porter's model will enable you to understand the industry you are or will operate in; it will help you describe the rivalry among competitors, the threat of new entrants in those markets, and the bargaining power of clients and suppliers as well as the substitute products to yours.

At the same time, you need to conduct a cultural analysis in order to understand all parties' cultures including your own. This will help you to better understand cultural stereotypes and go beyond them.

You should also conduct a SWOT analysis in order to identify real strengths and weaknesses from all parties and the market opportunities that could bring you together. In addition, identifying market threats can help you to fight common enemies. (For an extensive explanation about how to use these tools in international negotiation, read *The Intelligent International Negotiator*, Business Expert Press.)

Design Your Negotiating Strategy

Once you complete the market analysis and have a good understanding of what you can obtain from the negotiation, you need to design your negotiation strategy. To do so, you need to answer the following questions:

1. Why are you in this negotiation? What is your interest in the other company?
2. What is your main objective for this specific round? You may have secondary objectives leading to the main one.
3. Write down your concessions. Not all of them are strategic or important: no concessions, very high-value concessions, high-value concessions, or low-value concessions.
4. Consider the walk away situations.
5. Decide on your approach to sustainable negotiation.
6. Decide on your reactions to the other side's approach to see if it is win-win, win-lose, or sustainable.

Select Your Team Members

You need specific skills for specific negotiations. These will depend on hierarchy, technical skills, and soft skills;

Hierarchical alignment is important in several cultures even if high-ranked people are not really part of the negotiation but need to be there to show commitment and respect to the other parties.

Technical skills are needed when conversations are more specific regarding engineering, marketing, finance, production, and so forth.

Finally, the lead negotiator should be the one who has good soft skills, who is curious, likes meeting new people, and doesn't think that long conversations are a waste of time. This should be the person immersing the whole team into an intercultural situation and controlling the possible cultural blunders and missteps. They should be able to listen and observe at all rounds and to take over every time the negotiation drifts toward misunderstandings or potential conflict.

Schedule meetings with all the team members long before the negotiation round. Share information and make sure that everyone is aware of the negotiation goals and behavioral requirements. All team members should feel comfortable in their respective positions.

Don't bring to your team people who don't like to travel, are not curious, and have no patience with intercultural rituals.

Make the Needed Arrangements

If your team is the one traveling to meet the future partners, make all needed arrangements in advance. Book flights at convenient hours and comfortable hotel rooms. The hotel you stay in already tells about you.

Spare time for all your team members to rest, relax, and get rid of the jetlag before you start the negotiations. Allocate time to visit the surroundings and to get familiar with the local habits.

If you are hosting your future partners in your country, book a very good hotel where they can rest and relax. If they have a tough night, they won't be in good spirits to work with you the next morning.

Pick them up at the airport and drop them back there when they leave. Schedule dinners, lunches, and visits to the city. Also, allocate them free time and shopping time.

When you are hosting the meetings, you are responsible for their wellbeing. You need to look after them, mainly if this is their first visit and if they can't speak the local language. Everyone needs to feel welcome.

Part II
During the Negotiation

"Because we didn't have fear, we could do something drastic."
Masaru Ibuka, Founder of Sony Corporation

You and your business are not two separate things.

Chapter 4: Winning and Losing Are Just Emotions

As seen before, people tend to avoid tough conversations because they are stressful and unpleasant. That is why tough situations are often handled poorly. The use of electronic devices comes as a solution for that. Emailing and texting are used rather than face-to-face settings when approaching tough situations.

In international negotiation, working remotely has made it easier because it is also a way of avoiding the embarrassment of not knowing how to behave in other cultural settings. People would rather hide behind a screen.

But this easiness has a price – all non-verbal cues become invisible, which means that negotiators miss part of the information conveyed by others. It also means that it is impossible to build human and durable relationships without human contact.

The tricky aspect of this is that people think that, thanks to the distance, emotions are eliminated, but that is just an illusion. Emotions are inherent in people and they exist whether the exchanges are in person or remote. But people run away from emotions because they think they will lead to tough situations. This is a primary human reaction, as was the one from cavemen when facing danger. We either run away or fight. Run for your life!

In international negotiation, people don't run for their lives but often to save their honor. The issue is when stakes are high and emotions run strong, which is typically the case in international negotiations. When feeling in danger, people tend run or fight because the brain goes down to its more basic levels. The brain is drunk on adrenaline and people become blinded by their own emotions, losing control of what they say and do. Then, when the pressure goes down, they regret what they've done and/or said and it feels like a very bad hangover.

Often, when the goal is winning the negotiation, anger can take people beyond the desire of winning. Their goal turns into punishing and humiliating the other side. This has dramatic consequences at all levels.

Be Curious Instead of Furious

You can act on your emotions or be acted on by them. It all depends on the story you tell yourself, which creates your emotions. If you have decided to punish the other side, you will be against any solution or option they will come up with, even if some of them would be acceptable on your side. Although stories are not facts, your brain believes in the stories you are telling and take them as reality and so do you.

Shakespeare said that there is nothing *either* good *or* bad but thinking makes it so. Thus, winning and losing are emotions as much as joy, sadness, hope, despair, passion, and so forth. And emotions are temporary – now you feel like you won over someone but later on, it will feel like he/she's got more advantages than you. One of the main issues with win-win and win-lose negotiation strategies is that you can't know exactly what happened. It is just a feeling that is dissipated as soon as issues start. How and when can you state that you won or lost a negotiation? And how definitive is such situation?

Everything we do has an emotional weighting to it. No decisions are hundred percent rational. And your emotional state is conveyed to others whether you want it or not. Actually, people are a reflection of your emotional state. You can blame others, but they are more of a reaction to your emotional state than anything else. When you continuously re-experience the same emotions, you are caught in the same pattern of stimulus-response. This means that we always have a choice. The choice is also to be open to a new set of emotions. Typically, in negotiation, people are told not to feel or convey emotions. How can that be possible? Negotiators are people, and people are made of emotions too. In addition, if you have no emotions, how can you connect with other people? How can you empathize with them? Only via reason? That can't happen. Or is winning the only emotion acceptable in negotiations?

This is a very small window to what human interactions, including negotiations, are about. It is because we've been trying to turn negotiators in pre-programmed people that they fail so often. All they are told during trainings and from their bosses is, *"Be tough. Don't concede. Protect yourself. Don't feel emotions.*

Don't share information, and lie if needed. Take as much as you can and come back with a good deal for us."

If you always use the same emotions, your body gets addicted to them and will require that you feel them. That is why some people are always angry and complaining. Sometimes they don't really have any reason to complain and will get upset about something as minimal as, *"That mug is not at the right place."* Their brains are so addicted to anger that they feel the emptiness when it is not fed with anger for a while. They request their dose of anger. This is how people stay stuck in their anger and are unable to feel anything else. They are blind to other emotions. To them, life is made of anger.

As we saw before, preparing a negotiation requires time, effort, and energy. The more you will use your time to do daily and routinely tasks, the less time you will allow to be perfectible. It is exasperating to me to hear people saying that they had no time to prepare their negotiations. How come you don't have time to do your job? We know that there are no job positions for negotiators. That is why they don't allocate time to prepare their negotiations. Insofar businesspeople will keep improvising their negotiations, they will keep failing.

Companies should take international negotiations more seriously if they want to get to sustainable negotiation. Not having time to prepare your negotiations is as absurd as not having time to brush your teeth every morning. Not preparing your negotiations will lead to failures and frustrations very detrimental to your business. Your business will suffer from your negligence and be unhealthy until it shuts down. By not thinking in terms of future and not being ready for it in a sustainable way, you are signing the death sentence for your own business.

"Listen to people with original ideas, no matter how absurd it might sound at first."

McKnight, CEO of 3M

Chapter 5: Sustainable Negotiation Is a Mindset, a Lifestyle

In this lifestyle, the first step is to understand that in a sustainable world, you can live several lives in your lifetime. We all contain enough energy, talents, and interests to live many different types of lives, all of which could be authentic, interesting, and productive. There is no need to choose only one option and stick to it forever.

Life is a constant adventurous journey into the future with hopes, goals, helpers, unknowns, and serendipities, all unfolding over time. You need to build your life. And building is thinking. You build your strategy as the negotiation unfolds by thinking about the best options while building a relationship with your partners. It depends on you if this relationship will be good or bad for you and for them and how sustainable it can be.

Innovating and trying new and more appropriate strategies is not rocket-science. However, it scares more than one. Most people fail not for lack of talent but for lack of imagination. If you leave all options open to create your own reality instead of being subjected to it, it will flip you from judging to exploring – from negative to positive.

Your life will be much better if you live by the three golden rules of sustainable negotiation:

- Stay stuck in the past and you will perish.
- Be reactive and you might survive but you put yourself in constant stress.
- Be proactive and you'll lead the way.

Think about succeeding instead of winning. Aim at good decisions. And the best time to prepare is when you are not under stress. It is when you see beyond the obvious and get prepared to seize upcoming opportunities. Good decision-making and implementation leads to happiness and satisfaction because you succeed.

Everything in Life Is an Experiment

People like the freedom of choice. However, the more options we have, the more challenging and risky our decision can be. This takes us to paradox management. Dilemma is when you have two options and, to resolve this, you must pick only one. Paradox management occurs when you pick all options, without dismissing any of them, and are able to combine them, depending on the situation.

Often, we turn paradoxes into dilemmas because we think we must choose. You pick one option, and you are upset when your partners don't pick the same one. They want all options all the time and navigate among these.

Negotiators able to manage paradoxes don't see any valid reason to select just one. Why should they? Picking only one option makes them miss all the others!

The downside of abundant choice is that each option comes with a list of trade-offs. And trade-offs have psychological consequences– because you don't know what other opportunities you're missing. As a result, people might avoid making decisions because they don't want the risk of making the wrong one. Then they are seen as unskilled, unable to make decisions in cultures where people are respected because they are decisive.

Those frightened by the consequences of making a bad choice are not paradox managers. They just stand by to see what will happen and expect someone else to eventually make the decision for them. Making collective decisions is also a technique used by negotiators from several cultures. This implies shared responsibility if something goes wrong. Paradox managers are different. They decide to combine all options, according to the needs created by the context, as the negotiation evolves.

In all cultures, trade-offs bring confrontation and conflict. Conflicting options lead to the obligation of making choices. In contrast, embracing paradoxes is more comfortable than dilemma resolution because it circumvents the obligation of selecting only one option: the right one. Doing this is a challenge to randomness.

In an effort to increase the probability of finding the right option, decisions-makers follow the lead of patterns. This approach is reassuring and gives some tips about how things would be if the pattern occurs.

The Easiest Way Is Not Always the Best Way

You need to be able to let go the old patterns and fears. It is not easy, but it is not such a challenge either. Letting go is more of an inaction than an action. The action is finding the right path for you and for your business. Letting go opportunities because they didn't suit your interests is a wise thing to do. Focus on what is important and strategic to you. Don't let yourself be distracted with peripheral temptations. They will take you nowhere.

Most people take any opportunities that are flying around because they are scared of others' judgments. They might be seen as weak, unorganized, and risk-averse people unable to seize an opportunity. Indeed, for some people, missing an opportunity is seen as a sign of incompetence. Nothing could be further from the truth. There are thousands of opportunities showing up in the markets every day but they are not all for you. You can pick several of them but while you are busy with these ephemeral opportunities, you can be missing the real ones, the ones that are really for you and which will require your wit and undivided attention to turn into an asset for you. You'll be missing the sustainable ones.

Build a platform providing interactions to all actors involved. Instead of being limited to a negotiation, create an ecosystem where all parties can find the needed resources connecting suppliers, clients, lawyers, translators, and all of the people needed to get you to successful businesses.

Evolutionary Processes Can Be a Powerful Way to Stimulate Progress

We behave differently in different settings. Theories of negotiation don't take this into account. Neither do models of personality. They state that, "Whether we are introverted or extroverted, influence our behavior no matter the situation." Trait-based personality tests assume that we can be *either* extroverts *or* introverts but not *both*. But researchers know that the way we behave depends on *both* the individual *and* the situation. Rather than taking context into account, personality tests are all based on average scores.

But culture is all about context. The context principle is the opposite of essentialist thinking. While theorists were looking for behavioral consistency across situations, Shoda found out that an individual is consistent within a given context. Behavior cannot be explained or predicted without taking context in consideration. Behavior emerges out of the unique interaction between traits and the situation. Behavior is context-specific. Unpredictability comes by the fact that we don't think about this interaction between the individual and the context. We separate them as if they were not interdependent.

Thus, performance depends on context. Great examples of this are expatriates. They are expatriated because they are technically performant in their home companies. However, they are barely operational when they are required to do the same job abroad. If they are compatible with the host culture, they might perform well. Otherwise, they will have a hard time trying to do a job in which they excelled back home but not in the host country because they feel uneasy in the new environment. Our brain is sensitive to context and automatically adapts to the situation we find ourselves in. This explains consistency of behavior within same situations– fear when feeling threatened, happiness when feeling safe, shy with strangers, easygoing with friends, and so forth.

However, essentialist thinking still pervades every aspect of our lives and it is hard to resist the pull of false certainty. You need courage to try to swim in unknown waters. We think we know people because of the limited number of interactions we have with them, which is most probably always in the same context. It happens that we can be very surprised with the same peoples' behaviors when we take them out of that context. What is surprising to others' eyes can be just normal behavior of that individual in these types of situations. For example, you see a colleague you deem shy, because his behavior is more low-key at work, metamorphosed when dancing, making jokes, and having fun in a party. As you need to go back to what you know about him, you might be tempted to explain the situation based on futilities, such as the effect of alcohol or a willingness to show off... But you will not think that this is his habitual behavior in parties.

This also explains why in more contextual cultures, negotiators are taken away from the offices to social settings. The more you multiply the settings in which people behave, the more you can know these same people. Informal settings are meant to make people be more spontaneous and more genuine – to be who they really are. This is particularly useful in international negotiation because negotiators are taught to play roles at the table of negotiation. There is an impressive lack of sincerity and spontaneity. It is almost impossible to know who you are working with in these settings. As disruptive as it can feel to some negotiators to be invited to social events other than lunches and dinners, participating in weddings, birthday parties, or other social events are just as many occasions in which we can see how negotiators behave in different contexts.

Far too often, we interpret average patterns of behavior as proof that something is innate and universal, when in fact, the patterns might stem entirely from social customs that constrain what pathways are even possible in the first place. New theories undermine old ones because they enable people to break free of old fixed patterns. While we are talking about machine learning, we are preventing humans from learning from the context. Whichever their skills and capacities, we want them to fit into average patterns. That is a shame because every new path undertaken by an individual is an open access to infinite possibilities of progress and adaptability which unfold according to different situations.

The relationship between outside and inside factors has been known for centuries. Hippocrates, Galen, and other physicians before Paracelsus thought that disease was the result of an imbalance within the body, but for Paracelsus, disease resulted from a force that was outside the body. Later, the notion of contagious diseases confirmed the idea that what is outside peoples' bodies has an impact on them. All people don't have the same level of immunity and resistance to diseases. However, by being exposed to bacterial contagion, most people get sick.

Contagion also happens in social settings. When people are laughing, they make others laugh. When people are complaining, they make others complain too. Think about waiting rooms. At the beginning, no one talks to no one. Then, if one person starts complaining about how long this is taking and that they have other things to do the same day, everyone starts complaining too.

Be a Thought Leader

Imitating has never been a solution. Being a trendsetter means living your own life and not others' lives, as most people think. We presume that the best way to be performant, and thus be successful, is to walk in the footsteps of those who have succeeded. Benchmarking and imitation have tricked more than one. Because despite all we are told, the world and life are all but *one-size-fits-all*. Each individual has his/her way of performing and succeeding. We might learn the same techniques at school, but we use them differently. The ones who dare getting out of the well-blazed trail and do it their way have succeeded more often than those who stayed in the safe, well-known average standards. They think they'd better fit in normative thinking, which is true. The ones who do it differently surprise the markets, competitors, and partners. Because they go against what was expected, they take a unique position in the market. They are pioneers. And they succeed because they do it their way. They feel comfortable in the settings they created for themselves and this is why they excel in what they do.

The attempt of generalized obligation of squeezing everyone within the narrow walls of being average is not only an illusion but a lack of respect for each individual. We will never know all they can give because they are not allowed to do it differently. They might think differently, outside of the box as they say, but the settings they are in are so constraining that they can barely try to do things differently.

In today's patterns, we might preach creativity but there is no room for differences. No individual will ever give as much as they can because they are straightjacketed by rules that take all people down to being average and deliver expected behavior at work. This is also why we see them behaving differently in other settings than their offices. That is why most successful companies are individual-centric ones. The more individuals are valued for who they are and the ideas they have, the more committed they are to their companies. If they are able to execute their own ideas, their contribution to the company is much higher. They give the best they can.

Unfortunately, companies today still operate according to Taylorism, and to them, the system is more important than the individual and it compels the standardization of all processes. This also leads to the standardization of negotiating strategies. The cultural syndrome perspective views culture as influencing and activating cognitions and beliefs within specific contexts rather than as a motivation to perceive the world a certain way or to behave consistently across all contexts.

All negotiators are taught the same theories and play by the same rules. They all think they should win. If they don't win, they fail. Even when they have a great deal in their hands, but they didn't win. They compromised too much. If they don't get more than what they need, they lost the negotiation. This can only create frustrations in people who did a great job and reinforce the obligation of winning, which polarizes positions and creates distance between people. Instead of admitting interdependence, we create barriers between people who need each other.

Everyone uses the same strategies but want to obtain better results than the competitors. We can feel the weight of one-dimensional thinking that has become the norm. Artificially created scores and rankings for schools, companies, and countries are pervasive. They are arbitrary and inaccurate. The parameters defining success are also the same. These are the terms and the limits we set to ourselves. You cannot negotiate around the world only based on a couple of strategies developed in the 1980s.

We are not talking about future utopia here. This is a practical reality that can take companies to better business outcomes. Customization is the trend in B2C and it should also be in B2B when it comes to international negotiation.

How to Succeed with Sustainable Negotiation?

- Question your values without thinking about social desirability.
- Think reward rather than obligation.
- Don't drag things into the future that should be left in the past.

- Get rid of destructive thinking and aim at building something beneficial and sustainable. As much as positive thinkers are not dreamers, negative thinkers destroy positive reality.
- Let people do what they like to do and they will give you their best performance. You should love what you do too.
- Design your negotiating strategy. Getting to the negotiation table without thinking and planning upfront is highly risky. Don't count on luck.
- Time management is critical, as is organizing and planning. Use your time qualitatively. Sometimes lack of time is an excuse for not preparing the negotiation because people don't know how to prepare it and they get limited to price calculations. Then surprises happen when the negotiation is all but about price.
- Establish specific goals for each round.
- Review everything that happened during the round in the greatest detail. This should be the foundation to prepare for the next round.
- Establish goals for the next round based on that analysis.
- Evaluate what you've got back. Identify causes of failure and make the needed adjustments. Identify your blind spots.
- Continually assess your performance. This creates a constant state of improvement. Inspiration gets you started and habit keeps you going.

Chapter 6: Negotiation Is a Process

nternational negotiation, you can find different types of ple – the ones who enjoy the process of negotiating and se who want to have the job done at once and thus will ep the pressure on to speed up the process.

The ones who enjoy the whole process of negotiation ke their time. For them, the journey itself is the reward. generates constant motivation. Nothing is definitive and ll options stay open throughout the process. To them, egotiation is a conversation, a way of getting to know ach other, a basic human interaction. If you've been raveling to the Middle East as a tourist and tried to buy the simplest item, you know that it took you a while to check out. The conversation with the seller was endless but you ended up getting to know a new person and perhaps buying more than planned.

To the ones who want the job to be done at once, it is a challenge, a stressful situation, an obligation, and the sooner they sign a deal, the better negotiators they are. To them, collateral conversations and social events are a waste of time. If you've been buying anything in the United States, you know you'd better be ready very

- Visualize your negotiation. Your thoughts and actions create a pathway in your brain. By repetition, the pathway is strengthened and helps to do the task more easily.
- Establish clear and realistic goals for your first visit to your partners. Be prepared to behave accordingly.
- Allocate enough time to your trips. Don't rush anyone in a 2/3 daytrip. Most cultures need more time and local visits to establish trust. Allow yourself and your staff enough time to get rid of jetlag and to explore the surroundings before getting down to business.
- Invest in your negotiation rather than spend money on a trip – you need a comfortable, safe, and clean hotel for good night sleeps if you want to be in good shape for the following workdays abroad. Remember also that the type of hotel you stay in conveys an image of yourself and of your company.
- Listen and observe. Use all of your senses during the negotiations.
- Delegate – assign the right person to negotiate internationally. Don't send abroad someone who doesn't like to travel and who feels uncomfortable in unknown settings. Don't send unprepared people to negotiations. Don't get highly ethnocentric staff involved in intercultural interactions. Choose empathetic people instead.
- Don't be upset or disappointed when negotiators come back with no deals signed. Building trust

and relationships takes time. No immediate deal signed does not mean lack of progress.

- Yield to new habits. By doing so, you'll see your own evolution. Old habits will lose their controlling power and new habits will gradually form. Lasting success is never easy but it is possible. Failures are not easy either. Why endure them? Set your target on sustainable growth.

Remember to devote enough time to preparing your negotiation. If you are 'too busy' with other duties to focus on this preparation, it is because you don't take your own negotiations seriously. If you don't prepare, don't expect meaningful results. Give priority to what is strategic, not urgent or important.

If you let your routinely daily paperwork and less strategic tasks take most of the time you should allocate to preparing your negotiation, don't be surprised with the poor negotiation outcomes. And don't blame others for them. There are several paths to success as there are several ways to reach the same goals. If you don't prepare well enough, you might not see them all.

Creating the right environment to a succe.
is not an accident.

quickly, as the flow at the checkouts is meant to be very fast. It is a sign of good service and efficiency. Politeness is needed, but not long conversations.

Progress Is an Impulse for Activity

Design your strategy based on your vision of future and not on wining in the short term. It also means that you are making your choices of partners which fit in your values and with whom you can envisage a long-lasting relationship. Briefly said, it means that you know what you are doing without just imitating others or rushing to be the first one to innovating without really being ready for that.

You need time and genuine interest to build trust if you are to engage in a sustainable relationship with your partners. Trust is the last thing most people feel in a one-off negotiation. Each side is consumed with extracting the most value from the other: how to give up the least information so we can keep the most value to ourselves.

No wonder negotiators fail every day in their attempt to obtain better outcomes to their businesses both nationally and internationally. They focus more on how to attack others and defend themselves than on the essence of the negotiation itself, which is to obtain the needed resources to make their businesses sustainable. Honestly, no one creates a business with the intention to shut it down in few months or years. Everyone aims at having them around forever and eventually passing them on to the next generations. So why would negotiations stand on such short-termed patterns? Your partners are not your enemies.

They are the people who will help you to get to a better position in your markets. They are the ones who will help you to better satisfy your clients' needs and to consolidate your supremacy internationally. They are the people who will help you to beat your competitors.

That is also why most negotiators want to have a deal as soon as possible so that they don't need to face all the challenges of a long-lasting process. One of the ways of speeding up the process is keeping pressure on others. But it can backfire.

Where We Come from Decides Where We Go To

The theories in intercultural studies and cultural frameworks have not evolved much since the 1980s. The same can be said about the theories for negotiation. The theories of principled negotiation came as a breakthrough in the 1980s. Forty years later, professors, trainers, and negotiators around the world are still preaching and practicing the same theories as if the world hadn't changed meanwhile and as if the business landscape had not changed at all. New context, old theories! And are we supposed to be surprised that people fail their negotiations? With all the knowledge, advancement, technology, and globalization we have today, how can people fail their negotiations? One of the explanations to that comes from mismatched expectations. Businesspeople still think that all people are the same in the business world. They realize the hard way that there is a lot to be known about other cultures if they want to work with them. Globalization is a trap to negotiators.

Science has evolved and brought us new treatments and medicines, thanks to the discovery of new illnesses, and physics has gifted us with a better understanding of nature and the universe as much as new technologies have been developed to fulfill the need to know more. Yet, companies are using these new technologies with the wrong theories.

One of the main reasons for this lack of research and evolution in the understanding of international negotiation is the lack of job positions in negotiation. Did you ever see advertising for a company recruiting candidates for the international negotiator position? Of course not. People think that anyone in a company can negotiate, even internationally. Some companies think they are doing a great job when they pay someone to come over for a day or half-day to tell them about culture. The same kind of seminar is conducted in order to teach the staff how to become a tougher negotiator in order to win negotiations. And this is how they fail their negotiations when they face the real world of international negotiation. These inaccurate and improvised 'trainings' generate expectations that are unrealistic when it comes to face other negotiators in the international business place. They think they know and are well prepared but they are not.

In addition, books support such illusions. Most books about negotiation have been written by lawyers. They can be the best lawyers in the world but they are not businesspeople. They attended the law school and their expertise is in mediation, arbitration, and litigation, but not in business negotiation. Now take a look at the business schools. Do you see any major in international negotiation? You will see majors in marketing, finance, and accounting… but not in negotiation. As there are no job positions, there are no schools to educate international negotiators. And this is how they fail their negotiations.

Zoom out to Get Bigger Clarity

Although international negotiation has become trendy, it is not taken as seriously as it should be.

When I am asked to train teams on international negotiation in one day, or worse in a half-day, I can't have enough arguments to tell them this is just not possible. Sometimes they ask me to 'just give them the tools.' Sometimes it is 'just to encourage people to open up to other cultures.' If I accepted this kind of training, I would be dishonest and generate plenty of frustrations.

People asking me this have no idea of how much work and knowledge you need to be effective in international settings. Recent research in the intercultural field has started in the 1960s. How can we learn to master tools developed for more than fifty years in half a day?

It might be impossible to convert current negotiators to sustainable negotiators because they are more scared at novelty than at their poor results. And they refuse to predict the future of their companies, which depends on their own performance. But I am hoping that new generations of negotiators will have a better understanding of the contemporary needs and requirements of international negotiation. As per the words of Max Planck,

"A new scientific truth does not triumph by convincing its opponents and making them see the light, but rather because its opponents eventually die, and a new generation grows up that is familiar with it."

Just like for our planet, there is a lot of talking about sustainability, but little has been done. People keep going with their practices within their zone of comfort. Several summits have been held around the world and yet, not even participants to such summits can be viewed as role models when it comes to sustainability.

Most negotiators and theorists in negotiation still live in the past and their recommendations have probably worked out until the 1990s but are ineffective today. They are trying to fit a mammoth in a narrow drawer. Despite a considerable collection of failures, they keep reproducing the same old strategies and tactics, just like a machine that gives always the same answer no matter the questions you ask. It is like a robot vacuum that will hit the wall and keep going back and forth hitting the same wall over and over again. Even bugs learn faster with their failures. Whenever they hit an object, they learn to walk around it and keep moving forward. But humans don't seem to understand this so easily. They keep hitting the same wall over and over again no matter how badly it hurts.

Perhaps artificial intelligence will bring us a new generation of negotiators that can learn. If machines can learn, humans can too. They just need to want to learn. The main difference between machines and humans is commonsense. Unlike humans, machines don't have commonsense. If a computer can do what you do, it's because there is no need of thinking. As robots are programmable to do what they should do no matter what, learning machines will learn no matter what. There is no possible denial for robots. There is no power or pride preventing them from learning. This is the most threatening aspect of AI to people. Robots are not more intelligent, but they are certainly more disciplined and less fearful than humans, which makes them more efficient in some cases.

When the context changes, the core activities should change. We need to keep up with evolution. If technology is changing our lives, it is also changing our minds and practices. If cultures are interacting more frequently, it seems obvious that our understanding of cultures and intercultural interactions should be updated. Today, there is a huge gap between the technology used in the 2020s and the negotiation practices from the 1980s still preached by most theorists and practitioners. This is all incompatible. It is like wanting to ride a horse car in the middle of the highway.

Applying old solutions to new issues can be risky. It is the danger of *one-size-fits-all* thinking. Just because something worked in the past does not mean it will work today or in the future. Things change very quickly and fundamentally. So, beware of superficial similarities which can be hiding some deep differences.

Negotiators unable to adjust to the evolving environment will lag behind. Look at what happened to Turing, the inventor of computers. He was ridiculed and rejected by the scientific community because no one believed in the properties and benefits of computers. And look at us now. He was so disgusted to be humiliated that

- Visualize your negotiation. Your thoughts and actions create a pathway in your brain. By repetition, the pathway is strengthened and helps to do the task more easily.
- Establish clear and realistic goals for your first visit to your partners. Be prepared to behave accordingly.
- Allocate enough time to your trips. Don't rush anyone in a 2/3 daytrip. Most cultures need more time and local visits to establish trust. Allow yourself and your staff enough time to get rid of jetlag and to explore the surroundings before getting down to business.
- Invest in your negotiation rather than spend money on a trip – you need a comfortable, safe, and clean hotel for good night sleeps if you want to be in good shape for the following workdays abroad. Remember also that the type of hotel you stay in conveys an image of yourself and of your company.
- Listen and observe. Use all of your senses during the negotiations.
- Delegate – assign the right person to negotiate internationally. Don't send abroad someone who doesn't like to travel and who feels uncomfortable in unknown settings. Don't send unprepared people to negotiations. Don't get highly ethnocentric staff involved in intercultural interactions. Choose empathetic people instead.
- Don't be upset or disappointed when negotiators come back with no deals signed. Building trust

and relationships takes time. No immediate deal signed does not mean lack of progress.

- Yield to new habits. By doing so, you'll see your own evolution. Old habits will lose their controlling power and new habits will gradually form. Lasting success is never easy but it is possible. Failures are not easy either. Why endure them? Set your target on sustainable growth.

Remember to devote enough time to preparing your negotiation. If you are 'too busy' with other duties to focus on this preparation, it is because you don't take your own negotiations seriously. If you don't prepare, don't expect meaningful results. Give priority to what is strategic, not urgent or important.

If you let your routinely daily paperwork and less strategic tasks take most of the time you should allocate to preparing your negotiation, don't be surprised with the poor negotiation outcomes. And don't blame others for them. There are several paths to success as there are several ways to reach the same goals. If you don't prepare well enough, you might not see them all.

*Creating the right environment to a successful negotiation
is not an accident.*

Chapter 6: Negotiation
Is a Process

In international negotiation, you can find different types of people – the ones who enjoy the process of negotiating and those who want to have the job done at once and thus will keep the pressure on to speed up the process.

The ones who enjoy the whole process of negotiation take their time. For them, the journey itself is the reward. It generates constant motivation. Nothing is definitive and all options stay open throughout the process. To them, negotiation is a conversation, a way of getting to know each other, a basic human interaction. If you've been traveling to the Middle East as a tourist and tried to buy the simplest item, you know that it took you a while to check out. The conversation with the seller was endless but you ended up getting to know a new person and perhaps buying more than planned.

To the ones who want the job to be done at once, it is a challenge, a stressful situation, an obligation, and the sooner they sign a deal, the better negotiators they are. To them, collateral conversations and social events are a waste of time. If you've been buying anything in the United States, you know you'd better be ready very programmable to do what they should do no matter what, learning machines will learn no matter what. There is no possible denial for robots. There is no power or pride preventing them from learning. This is the most threatening aspect of AI to people. Robots are not more intelligent, but they are certainly more disciplined and less fearful than humans, which makes them more efficient in some cases.

When the context changes, the core activities should change. We need to keep up with evolution. If technology is changing our lives, it is also changing our minds and practices. If cultures are interacting more frequently, it seems obvious that our understanding of cultures and intercultural interactions should be updated. Today, there is a huge gap between the technology used in the 2020s and the negotiation practices from the 1980s still preached by most theorists and practitioners. This is all incompatible. It is like wanting to ride a horse car in the middle of the highway.

Applying old solutions to new issues can be risky. It is the danger of *one-size-fits-all* thinking. Just because something worked in the past does not mean it will work today or in the future. Things change very quickly and fundamentally. So, beware of superficial similarities which can be hiding some deep differences.

Negotiators unable to adjust to the evolving environment will lag behind. Look at what happened to Turing, the inventor of computers. He was ridiculed and rejected by the scientific community because no one believed in the properties and benefits of computers. And look at us now. He was so disgusted to be humiliated that

"A new scientific truth does not triumph by convincing its opponents and making them see the light, but rather because its opponents eventually die, and a new generation grows up that is familiar with it."

Just like for our planet, there is a lot of talking about sustainability, but little has been done. People keep going with their practices within their zone of comfort. Several summits have been held around the world and yet, not even participants to such summits can be viewed as role models when it comes to sustainability.

Most negotiators and theorists in negotiation still live in the past and their recommendations have probably worked out until the 1990s but are ineffective today. They are trying to fit a mammoth in a narrow drawer. Despite a considerable collection of failures, they keep reproducing the same old strategies and tactics, just like a machine that gives always the same answer no matter the questions you ask. It is like a robot vacuum that will hit the wall and keep going back and forth hitting the same wall over and over again. Even bugs learn faster with their failures. Whenever they hit an object, they learn to walk around it and keep moving forward. But humans don't seem to understand this so easily. They keep hitting the same wall over and over again no matter how badly it hurts.

Perhaps artificial intelligence will bring us a new generation of negotiators that can learn. If machines can learn, humans can too. They just need to want to learn. The main difference between machines and humans is commonsense. Unlike humans, machines don't have commonsense. If a computer can do what you do, it's because there is no need of thinking. As robots are in business negotiation. Now take a look at the business schools. Do you see any major in international negotiation? You will see majors in marketing, finance, and accounting... but not in negotiation. As there are no job positions, there are no schools to educate international negotiators. And this is how they fail their negotiations.

Zoom out to Get Bigger Clarity

Although international negotiation has become trendy, it is not taken as seriously as it should be.

When I am asked to train teams on international negotiation in one day, or worse in a half-day, I can't have enough arguments to tell them this is just not possible. Sometimes they ask me to 'just give them the tools.' Sometimes it is 'just to encourage people to open up to other cultures.' If I accepted this kind of training, I would be dishonest and generate plenty of frustrations.

People asking me this have no idea of how much work and knowledge you need to be effective in international settings. Recent research in the intercultural field has started in the 1960s. How can we learn to master tools developed for more than fifty years in half a day?

It might be impossible to convert current negotiators to sustainable negotiators because they are more scared at novelty than at their poor results. And they refuse to predict the future of their companies, which depends on their own performance. But I am hoping that new generations of negotiators will have a better understanding of the contemporary needs and requirements of international negotiation. As per the words of Max Planck, known about other cultures if they want to work with them. Globalization is a trap to negotiators.

Science has evolved and brought us new treatments and medicines, thanks to the discovery of new illnesses, and physics has gifted us with a better understanding of nature and the universe as much as new technologies have been developed to fulfill the need to know more. Yet, companies are using these new technologies with the wrong theories.

One of the main reasons for this lack of research and evolution in the understanding of international negotiation is the lack of job positions in negotiation. Did you ever see advertising for a company recruiting candidates for the international negotiator position? Of course not. People think that anyone in a company can negotiate, even internationally. Some companies think they are doing a great job when they pay someone to come over for a day or half-day to tell them about culture. The same kind of seminar is conducted in order to teach the staff how to become a tougher negotiator in order to win negotiations. And this is how they fail their negotiations when they face the real world of international negotiation. These inaccurate and improvised 'trainings' generate expectations that are unrealistic when it comes to face other negotiators in the international business place. They think they know and are well prepared but they are not.

In addition, books support such illusions. Most books about negotiation have been written by lawyers. They can be the best lawyers in the world but they are not businesspeople. They attended the law school and their expertise is in mediation, arbitration, and litigation, but not

They are the people who will help you to get to a better position in your markets. They are the ones who will help you to better satisfy your clients' needs and to consolidate your supremacy internationally. They are the people who will help you to beat your competitors.

That is also why most negotiators want to have a deal as soon as possible so that they don't need to face all the challenges of a long-lasting process. One of the ways of speeding up the process is keeping pressure on others. But it can backfire.

Where We Come from Decides Where We Go To

The theories in intercultural studies and cultural frameworks have not evolved much since the 1980s. The same can be said about the theories for negotiation. The theories of principled negotiation came as a breakthrough in the 1980s. Forty years later, professors, trainers, and negotiators around the world are still preaching and practicing the same theories as if the world hadn't changed meanwhile and as if the business landscape had not changed at all. New context, old theories! And are we supposed to be surprised that people fail their negotiations? With all the knowledge, advancement, technology, and globalization we have today, how can people fail their negotiations? One of the explanations to that comes from mismatched expectations. Businesspeople still think that all people are the same in the business world. They realize the hard way that there is a lot to be quickly, as the flow at the checkouts is meant to be very fast. It is a sign of good service and efficiency. Politeness is needed, but not long conversations.

Progress Is an Impulse for Activity

Design your strategy based on your vision of future and not on wining in the short term. It also means that you are making your choices of partners which fit in your values and with whom you can envisage a long-lasting relationship. Briefly said, it means that you know what you are doing without just imitating others or rushing to be the first one to innovating without really being ready for that.

You need time and genuine interest to build trust if you are to engage in a sustainable relationship with your partners. Trust is the last thing most people feel in a one-off negotiation. Each side is consumed with extracting the most value from the other: how to give up the least information so we can keep the most value to ourselves.

No wonder negotiators fail every day in their attempt to obtain better outcomes to their businesses both nationally and internationally. They focus more on how to attack others and defend themselves than on the essence of the negotiation itself, which is to obtain the needed resources to make their businesses sustainable. Honestly, no one creates a business with the intention to shut it down in few months or years. Everyone aims at having them around forever and eventually passing them on to the next generations. So why would negotiations stand on such short-termed patterns? Your partners are not your enemies.

Part III
After You Close a Deal

"You can't just keep doing what worked one time because everything around you is always changing."

Sam Walton

Chapter 7: Ideas Get Old

To be successful, you shouldn't have a love affair with old theories that have helped to win decades ago while your competitors are living forward. You don't want to be a follower. You want to take the lead, so you need to be ahead of your competitors. But you will never meet this goal if you stick with old theories.

Ideas as products are ephemeral; they can't be sustainable. But you want your company to shine forever even when you are gone. Bet on sustainable partnerships and development for that. Ideas are just market opportunities. You want your company to be more than that. Don't think product; think company instead. Don't negotiate for products. Negotiate for the future of your business. Aim at continuity rather than immediacy. This is what will set you apart from your competitors.

It was decided in the 1980s that there were only three types of negotiating strategies: accommodation (often used to renew existing contracts), distributive (also known as win-lose), and integrative (also known as win-win). As if these were not limited enough, they were presented as universal negotiating strategies without taking cultural differences into account. Nothing had been said about negotiating styles, cultural specificities, or simply about context. It is all linear and definitive. There is no need to look any further.

Whenever and wherever negotiation is taught today, it is limited to this theory. No one has ever bothered to look into international negotiation as if we were using a quantum telescope or microscope. All nuances and differences have been blurred by the certainty that this is how negotiation works around the world. Cultural frameworks based on research conducted with school teachers, students, managers, and others have been applied to negotiation a few times when someone in the room raises the issue of cultural differences. Or, dos and don'ts lists about dress codes and gift-giving habits are used when people go abroad for a negotiation. This is how limited the vision of international negotiation still is today. Negotiators see when they fail but never know exactly why they failed their negotiations. As they don't know, they can't learn from their mistakes and adapt their strategies. Thus, they keep using the same ones all the time because this is all they know.

Academicians proudly publish their research about negotiation in academic journals and it doesn't bother anyone that their results are based on data collected from students. Can we really compare a role-play about negotiation in a classroom with the aim of earning extra credit with negotiations in the real world where millions of dollars are at stake? This is how seriously the topic of international negotiation is taken. And these scholars are supposed to be experts in the topic. And the journals that accept such biased research for publication are the top-tier ones. That is, they are known as being the vectors of high-quality research. If you are a businessperson and follow their advice, chances are that you are going to do even worse than you would if you worked only based on your intuition.

Do it wrongly, and you will spoil your business. But would you really pay for an expert to customize a program to develop your business abroad? Or would you rather try to keep going with what you already know? How hurt should your business be before you realize that you are doing it the wrong way and that it is not the general context but your way of doing business that is taking you to bad outcomes?

Don't Be Your Own Victim

It is shocking the way companies deal with international business. It was more visible during the 2008 financial crisis. The first thing many companies did was to forbid travels to visit (potential) clients. All negotiations were done remotely. It is a fact that it saves money, but how can you build relationship through a conference call? You can't. Working remotely was also a way of avoiding the preparation to work abroad. It was a way to not to think about etiquette, language, food, dress code, and gift-giving, and avoiding all of the embarrassment traveling for business can engender when one is not well prepared. It was a very convenient shortcut to business. But it leads to short-term business, at best.

Now think of yourself as a client looking for suppliers. Most of them will tell you that you'll work remotely because 'you understand times are difficult for everyone...' But one of them comes to you and says that despite the difficult times, your business is a priority to them and this is why they came all the way to meet you in person. Who would your preference go to?

Nothing will ever replace human interactions at the level of in-person relationship building. No business relationship can be sustainable remotely. People need people to interact with and no technology can replace them.

If I tell you that I have been invited to weddings and birthdays by people I hardly knew when I was abroad, you might say that this is absurd because it has nothing to do with business. Well, it has, in their culture. What sounds absurd to you is just a habit to other people. Escher believed that 'only those who attempt the absurd will achieve the impossible.' Had I declined these invitations, I would certainly have fewer international clients today.

By creating boundaries between business and social life, several businesspeople are missing great opportunities. And by wanting to save time and focusing exclusively on business, they are turning into uninteresting people unable to talk about anything else than contracts. This makes them unprepared and tough negotiators to whom being nice equals being weak and accepting all invitations is being too obedient/tolerant.

Why should we always stress what won't work, what is complicated, and what can be tricky while none of these is necessary. It is much nicer to live in a nice world with nice people. If anyone accuses you of being too nice, tell them that such thing doesn't exist. You are a nice person or you are not. People confuse nice and weak in humans but not in objects, although the definitions are the same. Nice means beautiful, pleasant, and lovely, and weak means fragile. We like to look at nice objects and are careful with the fragile ones. Why would it be any different with people?

When talking about international negotiation, all we hear is that it is complex, stressful, conflicting, and time-consuming (in the sense of waste of time). But the same situation can be intriguing, compelling, fascinating, enriching, and enjoyable. As a matter of fact, most people accept stress as being an inherent part of international negotiation. Most stress comes from the fact that often negotiators are unprepared and culturally unaware.

Sometimes, it is this exacerbated level of stress that leads to failure. When you are stressed, you lose focus and have a hard time trying to work at high levels. You get tired more easily and have less concentration, mainly when you are abroad. You are also less confident and the other parties can sense it.

It all depends on how you build your negotiation. At least, this is my vision of international negotiation. Why? Because I left behind all of the old theories of fear and limited understanding of negotiation and intercultural interactions to give it a brand-new and unique perspective – a sustainable one.

How did I get there? I am curious. I like to get to know new people and new places. I enjoy learning from others as much as I enjoy conveying to others what I have learned. Because of this, I spontaneously got into sustainable relationships with my clients and partners. I enjoy negotiating because I don't put myself in a stressful situation uselessly. I don't feel threatened by the people I want to work with. I am nice to them and they are then nice to me. You harvest the fruits of your own seeding. And I am always well prepared. You are never over-prepared.

Get Ready for the First of Many Successful Negotiations

If you are tired of failing your negotiations, of not knowing why you fail them and of wasting money with unfruitful relationships, turn to sustainable negotiation.

Sustainable negotiation is a theory I coined in 2017 as a much comfortable and efficient way of negotiating internationally. As much as we need to think about the sustainability of our planet's resources, we need to think about the sustainability of our businesses. If you want to sustain growth, you need to choose the partners that will help you to get there. No business grows alone today. And you should not fight your potential partners during the negotiations because you need them to grow. You should build business with them. That is why it is so important to carefully choose the people you can work with for long.

One on the pillars of sustainable negotiation is the understanding that negotiation is not an act, as it has been defined by several authors in the past. Negotiation is a process, a big one, which doesn't finish when a deal is signed. The after-deal is as important as all the phases of your negotiation. The after-deal is when you actually work with your partners. It is the daily life together and the path you will follow together to reach the growth you aim at.

But growing is not enough; you need to be able to sustain such growth. Anyone can grow once or twice, but how do you perpetuate it? If you are experiencing ups and downs all the time, your strategy is inefficient. It is probably short-term-oriented. To sustain growth, you need to have a sustainable relationship with your partners. You need to grow together. The how, who, and when are to be established prior to signing any deal so that the after-deal can be carried on in a smoother fashion.

Preparation is paramount. You need to conduct your cultural analysis before even starting to exchange emails and phone calls with your potential partners. You need to design your strategy by using all tools that are at your disposal. See the 'international negotiator toolkit' in *The Intelligent International Negotiator* book.

Forget about the win-win strategy. It is just an illusion. Or do you really think that there can be more than one winner in a competition? And if you use a win-lose strategy, forget about sustainability. No one who lost to you will wish to work with you again. The same applies to you if you are the one who lost. If anything, win-win and win-lose are short-term tactics, not strategies.

Forget about identifying other party's personality or other advices that abound in trainings and on the internet. You know very well that this is not possible. Instead, get to know their culture and their negotiating styles. You can find all details in *Sustainable Negotiation. What Physics Can Teach us About International Negotiation.*

But all these will be worthless if you don't have the right mindset. More than anything else, sustainability is a state of mind. It is a lifestyle. It is a specific perspective to life, people, and things that surround us. It is a vision of future with no term. It is also the opposite of everything we have been taught so far.

Don't Be a Conversation Narcissist

Most negotiators tend to not listen to their partners' issues and concerns. They usually take them as a counterargument or as an excuse not to agree with their terms readily. They want to talk about themselves and their interests in this negotiation. Be wiser than them. Let your partners talk and join in. Remember that their problems become your problems if they are in the way to an agreement. Don't close the door to such a precious source of information. You need this information. People like to talk about themselves and favor people who listen to them. How can you build a sustainable relationship with anyone without listening and empathizing? As much as you would join your partners in an activity (often golf), you need to join them in their issues and concerns.

Listen. Listen to what the markets are telling you. Listen to what your clients tell you. Listen to any person who could be your potential partner. Take off your headset and listen to people, to real people in the real world.

Real progress has been made by new generations of physicists, less set in their ways and less committed to old ideas, fired by new discoveries in atomic radiation and looking for new answers to both old and new questions. Let's take our inspiration from them.

The complete break with classical physics comes with the realization that not just photons and electrons but all particles and all waves are in fact a mixture of wave and particle. While Dirac made quantum theory more abstract and cut it free from everyday physical ideas, Schrödinger tried to restore easily understood physical concepts, describing quantum physics in terms of waves, which are familiar features of the physical world. However, he fought to the end of his life the new ideas of indeterminacy and the instantaneous jumping of electrons from one state to another.

There is a simple way to explain sustainable negotiation, provided you are prepared to abandon the ingrained ideas of traditional negotiation techniques and cultural frameworks and to open up to new standards in international negotiation.

International negotiators might eventually get there, hopefully I would say. The main issue is that students raised on those texts become, in some cases, professors in their turn and pass on the same beliefs to subsequent generations. Or they get positions in companies after they graduate and use the theories about negotiation they learned from their teachers. It perpetuates the old ideas of negotiation which are inappropriate to the contemporary reality of international business.

Time is upon us and businesses need to be updated because markets' volatility is increasing. There is a lot going on in the world in politics, economy, social settings, and science. We can't wait centuries to figure things out.

Market concentration is happening right now and this is when you pick your partners. Think about yourself in a dance party. If you don't pick your dance partner now, you will end up dancing with the one you didn't want to dance with. Or you'll sit alone all night long.

More than thinking about winning, you should focus on growing with the right partners for you. Winning is hazardous and a short-termed vision of business. Most negotiators relay too much on luck. Every time they take a negotiation as a game, their chances of failure can overweigh their chances of success because they can hardly control the outcomes of a game.

Problems are opportunities for evolution.

Chapter 8: It Doesn't Need to Be Perfect, It Needs to Be True

In international negotiation, you negotiate on behalf of the company you work for. There is a lot at stake – money, competition, and possibly your job. If you aim at winning, you are envisioning your negotiation as a game or a fight. You can *either* win *or* lose. You are adding even more uncertainty to your endeavor.

If you get to your negotiation with the willingness to see what you and your partners can build for the future and adjust to each other as the process unfolds, you are positioning your negotiation at much higher levels than just a game or a fight. This way, there are much more controllable than uncontrollable variables in your negotiating process. Games and fights are short-termed activities. What you want is a lasting relationship to take you and your business to sustainable growth.

You keep interacting with your potential partners throughout the whole process of sustainable negotiation. This is why you can control several factors and can handle several options at the same time. There is more than winning or losing in negotiation. You are shaping your relationship as well as the future of your business. Let me take you back to physics for a moment to better explain the function of interactions.

Whereas in classical physics we imagine a system of interacting particles to function like clockwork regardless of whether or not they are observed, in quantum physics the observer interacts with the system to such an extent that the system cannot be thought of as having independent existence. By choosing to measure position precisely, we force a particle to develop more uncertainty in its momentum, and vice versa. By choosing an experiment to measure wave properties, we eliminate particle features because no experiment reveals *both* particle *and* wave's aspects at the same time.

This holistic vision in which the parts are in some sense in touch with the whole is indispensable in sustainable negotiation. We don't negotiate for something specific but for a future together, for a relationship which will bring us most of what we need. It is not about selling/buying a single product. It is about how bringing our resources together will lead us to sustainable growth. To do so, we need to be open to all possibilities. The world seems to keep all its options, all its probabilities open for as long as possible; we do the same in sustainable negotiation. Limiting the options since the beginning limits the possibilities of partnerships. This narrows down to what is accepted to be possible while what is real still exists. Nothing is real unless we look at it, and it ceases to be real as soon as we stop looking. It is not because you don't see it that it doesn't exist.

In the international negotiation world as much as in the quantum world, everything we call real is made of things that cannot be regarded as real. What we see is what we get. "Nothing else is real," as Bohr used to say. We, humans, are limited to what we want to see as real. But reality goes far beyond what we can see; we just need to look at it. When you see human behavior, you don't see the internal mechanisms that make people behave the way they behave. You just see their behavior which becomes real to you. That is why sometimes you don't understand peoples' reactions. This often happens in international settings. We can't see culture, but we can see how people behave in certain cultures. And sometimes we are surprised, scared, and intrigued because their behaviors are inconsistent with what we know as being normal or right. The explanation to that is that cultural rules differ from culture to culture.

Everything in the macroscopic world is made of particles that obey the quantum rules. And every person in a given culture is taught and required to behave by its specific cultural rules. It is just that the rules are different in different cultures.

People Are Poor Communicators

Don't be one of them. Listening and observing are key factors in international negotiation and yet we are not taught to do so. If you attended a business school or were trained by businesspeople, you were taught to talk, to persuade, and to convince. You can talk as much as you want, but it will be useless if no one listens to you, if what you say is not what they want to hear, and if they can't understand what you are saying. In addition, talking is not conversing. Conversation is interaction, which is not talking.

If you don't listen, you don't know. If you don't observe, you don't know. If you don't listen, you miss the verbal part of the information. If you don't observe, you miss the non-verbal part of the information. In any case, you are missing relevant information to establish whichever kind of relationship you want to establish with other people, let alone a sustainable one. To get into a sustainable relationship, you need to know and to let know.

D'Espagnat says that our everyday view of reality is based on three fundamental assumptions. First, that there are real things that exist regardless of whether we observe them; second, that it is legitimate to draw general conclusions from consistent observations or experiments; and third, that no influence can propagate faster that the speed of light, which he calls locality. Together, these fundamental assumptions are the basis of local realistic views of the world.

If you want to have a more realistic view of the people you want to do business with, you need to take your time to listen and observe. The people you are negotiating with are a primary source of information. They will tell you things you'll never find anywhere else, and certainly not on the internet. They will disclose the kind of information that is only disclosed in person. That is why no technology will ever replace human interactions. Working remotely seems more comfortable and cost-efficient but only in the short term. It gives a false idea that everybody behaves the same way in a conference call despite the distance and culture.

Sustainable negotiation establishes rules that will take you to a very different world view from that of our everyday common sense. Common sense is needed, but it is not enough to get there. You need to know how other people see reality and future if you want to undertake a sustainable business with them. Here again, I mean a holistic view of these people, not only what products they can sell or buy and at which prices. Sustainable negotiation requires more information and deeper understanding of underlying values and practices.

Sometimes it might feel like what some people do and the way they think don't make much sense. It looks paradoxical and you end up highly confused. You are probably facing a paradox. Feynman used to say, "Paradox is only a conflict between reality and your feelings of what reality ought to be." Thus, anything different from what you think reality is or should be is disturbing to you. The only way of avoiding this level of disruption is to know upfront that different visions of reality exist. What's more? Different realities exist.

Luck Favors the Persistent

What make our lives are the choices we make. And these choices are based on our beliefs. It is not chance that selects the conditions suitable for life out of the array of quantum possibilities but choice. There are many options out there. Some time ago, physicists decided to make their choices about whether accepting the Copenhagen interpretation of the quantum world, with its ghost realities and half-dead cats, or accepting Everett's interpretation of many worlds. They can be *both* right *and* both wrong.

However, what can be wrong now can be proven right in few years. History of science has proven this throughout the centuries. There is no absolute right or wrong. What can be right in your culture can be wrong in mine and conversely. The choices we make should just be suitable to our aims. We build our own reality by the choices we make both in our personal and professional lives. The choices we make not only shape our present but also our future. We rarely realize that.

With the evolution of science emerge puzzling ideas. There are no fundamental answers to all of our questions yet, but it does no harm to know that our understanding of several phenomena is still confused and uncertain. It broadens the mind to contemplate that if the theories we understand break down, the progress is likely to come from things we don't yet understand.

In addition, there are no answers where there are no questions. There is only one way to know and it is asking questions. Getting used to always do the same things is more comfortable than being efficient.

Don't forget to be human.

Chapter 9: Engage with Empathy

It is the interaction between the foreigner and the locals that creates the situations which are often described as typical behaviors in that culture. This is a false assumption because all you can say about people from another culture is how they behave while interacting with you. You can't know how they behave when you are not there.

When it comes to sustainable negotiation, we can also think about how we are going to behave with each other in order to work together. We create our own work culture so that no one's culture takes over the other ones and everyone can feel comfortable with the standards we have established together.

More often than not, books and trainings about culture focus on culture shock or collision as being something we should fear or even avoid. In physics, when matter and antimatter collide, they neutralize each other and release enormous energy. This is how sustainable negotiation works. Creating a work culture that enables people to work together for a long time is the key to sustainable negotiation. And the fact that cultures are different adds value to the negotiation because different points of view and practices can well be complementary rather than conflicting. Opposites can attract each other just like poles in nature. After a while, it was discovered that atoms with positive and negative charges could come together as for H_2 or O_2, which didn't seem to make sense before and had been neglected for several years. We know now that it was true. This reinforces the notion of endless possible options. In nature, *both* positive *and* negative poles can come together. The same holds true to cultural interactions.

Creating a work culture can be inspired by the principles of conservation of parity. The principle of conservation of parity states that a mirror-reversed universe is physically possible. In several equations, all remains the same if we reverse them. Parity comes from what is given away and what is taken in negotiations. You can reorganize your business in a way that will make it more profitable without giving up on your culture and your values while benefitting from your partners' practices and ideas.

The Search for a Unified Theory

From Descartes who said that vacuum was impossible to the tortured development of the unified field theory from its primitive origins, the superstring theory of today resembles in some sense the twists and turns found in a good mystery novel as described by Kaku. The main aim of contemporary physicists is to find a theory for everything, which was also the main fundamental research conducted by Stephen Hawking. The more interconnected the universe appears to them, the more scientists believe in a possible unifying theory.

As much as there is excitement generated by new discoveries, this doesn't mean that a new unified theory will be readily accepted by the scientific community. It could be an answer to the questions posed by the Greeks several thousand years ago. However, one reason why remarkable achievements have not won instant recognition is that usually some people are ahead of their time. These people are visionary and set the stage for breakthroughs years or even decades before their realization by others.

Sustainable negotiation resembles to the physics' unified theory. It brings people, cultures, practices, and objectives together. It is like creating a work platform in which businesspeople will find the resources they need to propel growth. It is sustainable because it goes far beyond the material products companies buy from each other. It is a group of companies you share values with and take as partners just like when you create your group of friends. You are not friends with people you have nothing in common. And friends are forever, but they are all different and you don't practice the same activities with each one of them. However, there is something that brings them together and makes them stick together. There is loyalty because there is understanding and adaptation to each other. You take your friends as they are because you respect them. You can do the same with your business partners, exactly the same. You just don't need to love them!

What you build with the people you choose to be part of your personal life is meant to last. You should do the same with your business partners.

Sustainable negotiation is not just a set of techniques but an entire mindset for turning complicated problems into simple solutions. If you let opposed facts or solid judgments overwhelm your experience, common sense, and your willingness to do better business, you might be disappointed with your results.

Regardless of your position in a company or organization, there is always a flood of information, data, and a lot of conflicting ideas and opinions. How you get to the heart of what matters will define you as a competent negotiator. Sustainable negotiation aims at facilitating this process.

Sustainable growth is not only for leaders. You should know how to avoid the yo-yo cycle. Just like in a diet, you need to avoid the yo-yo growth. Anyone can achieve a onetime score. Success can be just a moment–a big gain that brings high praise. Achieving further and sustainable goals are something else as stated by Kilts. But rollercoaster growth will hurt you and your company. Businesses need negotiators who are predictable in their ability to deliver sustainable growth.

Lasting success is never easy but you need to stick to timeless strategies if you want to propel growth. Focus on what you want to be and then design the right strategy to get there. Move relatively to your markets and competitors. These are the factors you need to size up. The theory of relativity laid down by Einstein stated exactly this – all movement is relative. It can only be measured in relation of something else.

Kilts has asserted that you must anchor your plans on rock-solid fundamentals, the most important of which is assessing the right rate of revenue growth. Bloated estimates, broken promises, and a string of bad business practices are ways of wiping out a company's credibility and making any turnaround a difficult feat.

When you identify the fundamental concepts that will drive your performance, you need to stick to them. But first make sure that these are really fundamental because all your strategy will be based on them. They should be long-lasting too. The future of your business depends on this.

Portray Your Business's Personality

Success in business demands that you comprehend and confront the reality of your business situation. Without a full and honest assessment, your basis for action is flawed from the start and future actions will suffer. It underscores the difficulty of confronting reality and the importance of an unbiased pre-assessment. Think about physicians. The first thing they do with their patients is a diagnosis after which they are able to prescribe a treatment. If the diagnosis is wrong, the treatment will be wrong. You should do the same constantly. Don't take your business for granted. The knowledge you think you have is not enough and will never be. You need to know not to assume.

Many companies are culturally and organizationally hardwired in a way that makes it difficult to say, "This isn't working. We have to start again and differently." It is also a matter of pride and of lack of confidence. If you focus more on your reputation and what people will think of you, you will never reach sustainability. Your actions will be based on shallow and short-termed rather than fundamental drivers. If you think that rethinking, challenging, and reviewing what you have been doing is a sign of weakness, you are already on the wrong path to sustainable growth. Businesses should be reinvented every day. This means vision, not instability. This means trying to do even better every day. Doing 'just fine' is not enough.

Most companies get into trouble not because they make world-class blunders but due to a succession of well-intentioned yet flawed decisions that build on one another until much larger problem is created that is extremely difficult to unravel. As an international negotiator, you are a problem-solver. Your job is to take your business to higher levels of competitiveness not to create new problems by never questioning the wrongs and the rights you have done. Some problems need immediate solution; some are predictable and thus avoidable. Your job is to eliminate the blind spots and anticipate what is going to happen in the markets and get your business ready for it. Everything happens for a reason and you need to identify that reason.

Don't Feel Like You're Left Out

Don't think of sustainable negotiation as an action but as a shift in perspective. If you are in the right frame of mind, your actions within that frame will be consistent.

Shift just like history or science. Before Newton, all events were explained as being acts of God. Before Darwin, we would say of animals and plants that they were as they were, without thinking why they were as they were. Thanks to Darwin, we learned about genetic code, mutations, natural selection, adaptation, and evolution of species. You can't keep repeating and reproducing what no longer works. You need to shift to another perspective and look for better ways to seize the best opportunities for you.

And remember that being successful is not enough – it needs to be sustainable. For you to be successful as a negotiator, you should first understand the overall market, the products you are competing against, the consumer dynamics of the product category, how consumers view your brand, and the value they attach to it. This might sound as being a basic rule, which is unfortunately all too often ignored at many companies. They take their market for granted.

They will tend to focus on the financial department and procurement rather than listen to the market. But the basic understanding of a company is that the clients are the ones who bring the money. Money flows where the focus is. With no clients, there is no need of financial and procurement departments. No clients, no money, no company.

Embracing Change

To succeed, you need to stay out in front of that change rather than be a follower of, even worse, a laggard. Shifting is being curious and adventurous. Staying in the comfort zone does little to stimulate progress. And progress doesn't just show up. You are responsible for making progress. You are the one who needs to know the answers to these questions.

Where are you taking your business to? How clear do you have the path you are undertaking? And with whom are you going to walk towards your goals? Why? What do you know about these people and what do they know about you? Do you know who you are and who you want to be? These are fundamental questions you should ask yourself before choosing your partners.

Knowledge is the key. Most people fail in the business place because they think they know. They forget (refuse) to look into all they don't know. Look at all the evolution of science discussed in the previous pages. We always thought that we knew, and we didn't. The assumptions were wrong, the intuitions were inhibited, and the freedom of speech was forbidden. We are lucky that now we have tools to know. You should use them for your own good.

You need the right information and knowledge of several markets to project your business into the future. How will external environment change? What will you need to put your organization in the best position to prosper? Who can provide you with what you need today and in the future?

Your best solution is to work with a company with similar vision, values, culture, and the scale and resources that would enable both companies to grow and to go head-to-head with the most powerful competitors. Aren't you better off initiating the negotiating process with your partner of choice when you're working from a position of strength than waiting to be picked up by someone when something has gone wrong and you are operating from a position of weakness? You can always do better. It all depends on your business philosophy. It shapes the market and practices. Look for a sense of common purpose.

Being strong today doesn't imply being strong tomorrow. How can we explain so many bankruptcies and companies going out of business? If we leave apart poor management, corruption, and politics, we'll find out that one of the main reasons for failure is a lack of leadership and of a vision of future, a lack of understanding of the markets' evolution, a lack of preparation for what was coming, and too much confidence on past accomplishments.

You need to be ambitious but realistic. You must spend time in identifying a rate growth that is realistic and sustainable for your sector and business, and not just for a year or two, but for the future. Remember that the future has no term. Setting a sustainable growth target is one of the most important things you can do. What's needed is a multidimensional effort. The company's culture must change. Many behaviors must be unlearned. Future-oriented thinking and sustainable competitive advantage must drive all efforts. Your roadmap needs initiatives to achieve top capabilities.

The key is to not put boundaries where they don't exist. We live in a vast universe and the options are countless. Search for the best ones for you without being limited to what you can see from a narrow window. Aim different!

Knowing what not to do is as important as knowing what to do.

Chapter 10: Beyond the Deal

This book is meant to give you a different and better perspective for your business, thanks to sustainable negotiation. The relationship between international negotiation and science is a way to show you that what seems to be totally unrelated is in fact interconnected. What happened in sciences happens in culture and in business.

Set your business free from the mind-control cult. This way of having everyone doing the same things the same way will take you nowhere. You should take control of your business to shape it the way you want it to be. Be your business designer. Let your competitors believe and practice win-win while you will be the one creating your future in a sustainable way. Let them be the losers in the future. Let them be stuck with the remaining options while you will have already chosen the best partners to ensure your sustainable growth.

If you do this, you won't even need to challenge your competitors, as they will naturally fall one by one because their short-termed visions will lead them eventually to failure. Instead, you will be shining in the marketplace with the best hires and partners. You will be what you want to be rather than what you could be, or what the markets will allow you to be. Sustainable growth will bring you loyalty from your customers, partners, and shareholders. This can only reinforce the sustainability and the value of your business.

Would You Like to Work with Yourself?

When negotiating internationally, you might find people who understand your goals and your vision of future – put in a simple way – people who understand what you say. These are the people you want to work with in a sustainable way. They can bring you as much as you can bring to them and this is not limited to products. Don't think products or services; think resources. But you need to give them good reasons to want to work with you too.

Beliefs lead to certainties which lead to false assumptions. Many people think that their thoughts are truth while they are just their own perception of truth. Then they are disappointed when reality shows them something different. They get into cognitive dissonance which is very uncomfortable because people don't like to face contradictions. They want their assumptions to be confirmed by reality. It is very disrupting to international negotiators to face unexpected behaviors once they are at the table of negotiations. This is when reality hits them. Had they disrupted from old and well-settled beliefs when preparing their negotiations and replaced their assumptions with information, their journey abroad would have been much more pleasant.

You can turn your hopes into reality but it should come from you. Don't expect that to just happen if you don't get involved in creating your own reality. You are an actor of your reality and of your future. You decide today who you'll be tomorrow and this has nothing to do with luck. It has to do with choices and actions. It all depends if you decide to be a dreamer or a problem solver. You can be a dreamer as long as you are able to turn your dreams into objectives and go for them. And as a sustainable negotiator, you are a problem solver. You solve current problems by looking for the right resources and you anticipate problems in order to avoid them. This is the vision of future you should have. In doing so, you are shaping the future of your business.

Criticism Can Lead to Progress

Unraveling problems is indispensable but anticipating them is wiser. You need to size up your competitors and the challenges and the opportunities the markets will offer to build a sustainable business. Only dealing with the most pressing issues won't take you to a higher level. You will be always busy catching up on current issues instead of projecting yourself in the future. You need to set your targets on a timeline with no deadline and identify the resources you'll need to get there. Then, you need to identify the people who can provide you such resources and go negotiate with them. If you stay anchored by traditional solutions, you will be less creative and less visionary. You will just keep trying to do better next time. Get away of tentativeness and go where you can really get things done. Set the stage for better business rather than just complying with the hazardous orientation and options markets are giving you. You are not supposed to be subjected; you are supposed to make it happen.

If you don't have the knowledge and the time to turn yourself into a skilled sustainable negotiator, look for people who are specialized in sustainable negotiation. They will be your partners as much as your suppliers and clients and will help you to find the right resources to grow durably. The same way you hire a lawyer for your business, you should hire professionals specialized in international negotiation to help you out with your endeavor.

Think of the markets as a wave as do physicists. Your particle will be somewhere in this wave but you can't know exactly where because there are fluctuations. But you want to keep it in that wave. Your particle is your business in the markets which fluctuate for several intrinsic and extrinsic factors. You want to stay in this market and keep growing within it. You will never know exactly where you are but you know that all your actions increase the probability of keeping your business in this wave.

You should co-create your future. Contracts are static. Relationships are dynamic. For your company, you might just seize the existing opportunities with some available partners in the market or create your own future with the partners you choose now. Co-creating the future of your company implies constant interactions with your partners while shaping the future you envisage for your company. It is all based on sustainable negotiation.

While listening and observing are indispensable, make sure that you are learning from that. Collecting information is just the first step to understanding. It all depends on how you process the information and how you use it.

If You Act as a Barbarian, You Become a Barbarian

Think of after-deal to be sustainable. Remember that famous bid in Wall Street in the 1980s – RJR the company owning Nabisco and Reynold's was purchased by KKR in one of the biggest bids in the history of Wall Street. All candidates to the acquisition went through very tough negotiations. At the end, it had become a matter of pride to win it. Yes, their only goal was to win the negotiation.

But, not surprisingly, after the purchase, the company went downhill and few years later, Philips Morris purchased the tobacco branch of the group. The new CEO of Nabisco spent the four-billion-dollar reserve put away by the former CEO in a few months. It was said that he had more faith in his MBA degree and little sense for the pitfalls of their real-world applications.

Unlike their competitors, Nabisco used to have a direct-to-store approach, distributing their products with their own trucks and having them placed on the shelves by the company's employees. Not knowing what to do, the new CEO hired McKinsey to help him cut costs. They got rid of the distribution channels, and consequently their clients were furious because they had built a long-term relationship with Nabisco's employees. Now they had impersonal business with the company. Their orders would go through some intermediaries with whom they would negotiate the prices. As a result, Nabisco's products' space on retailers' shelves was reduced. Few years later, the whole company was sold for much less than its real value.

This is a lesson to learn. KKR won the negotiation but didn't know how to run the company after the deal was closed. The staff at KKR was of lawyers. They didn't know how to run a company in the FMCG (Fast-Moving Consumer Goods) market. They hired unprepared people to run the company for them, which was a bad choice. But the worst decision they made was terminating the sustainable relationship that had been established between the company and its clients for so long. Their short-termed vision turned what was supposed to be an investment into a waste of money and loss of value for the company. All this happened because their only goal was to win the negotiation and had no vision of how the after deal would shape up.

Be a Sustainable Negotiation Genius

Researchers came up with a typology of minds. There are people with fixed minds who would rather stick with fixed routines to avoid challenges and those with growth minds who find challenges invigorating and thus engage in the process of constant learning. They are curious, and improvement at all levels of their lives is their main motivation.

Having a performant team of international negotiators in your company starts with the choice of people you make. Those with fixed mind can be excellent in home and routine negotiations such as deal renewals with already well-known partners. But they will be very unsuccessful if you send them abroad. They like routine; this is their zone of comfort and this is where they excel. Pushing people out of their zone of comfort is only optimized if they don't feel too threatened. Otherwise, they are paralyzed by panic and you'll get the opposite outcome.

International negotiators who perform well are those who are energized by curiosity, new challenges, and new perspectives. These are the people who should be trained and prepared to be negotiators. Their minds are already set to accept and understand the joy of discovery. They don't fear failures because people with growth minds take failures as part of the learning curve.

The scientists and high-achievement people mentioned in this book were not all geniuses and they all experienced failures. But what they had in common was curiosity, perseverance, and motivation to learn.

When designing your plan for growth, don't think quantitatively. Numbers will come up as a consequence of quality. Think more about where and how rather than how much. Your gains will be as sustainable as the what-you-want-to-be-in-the-future and the how-you-get-there are sustainable.

Commit to incremental improvement and let your questions create the path for your actions. The right questions you'll ask yourself will keep you on the right track.

Sustainable negotiation can be achieved with method by anyone who perseveres. You shouldn't do it tentatively but assertively. You need to believe. While others fear the future, you shape yours. Take action today and be in control of your future. Identify your strengths and how you can use them to shape and seize future opportunities.

Now articulate your strengths with those of your (potential) partners to seize future opportunities. How much better can you do it than alone?

Stop being a generalist and become a specialized sustainable negotiator. It is a full-time job. You need to monitor markets and identify possible partners and future competition. You need to keep up with cultures' dynamics and evolution and prepare your negotiating strategies. And you need to sustain your relationship with your partners. Your successes and failures all come down to your actions.

And What If?

The final thoughts for you as this book reaches its end are to consider the following options:

- What could go wrong if you tried sustainable negotiation instead of what you practice now?
- What could go wrong if you didn't undertake a sustainable negotiation approach?
- Are your actions due to habit or are there legitimate reasons for them?
- How much time do you spend in activities that are valuable to your business and your career?
- Do strategic activities take at least sixty percent of your time?

- Do you have a program to achieve your goals of sustainable growth?
- How do you intend to reach a bright future without engaging in sustainable negotiation?

Finally, don't prevent yourself from taking the qualitative leap to get quantum rises in the quality and quantity of your results.

"We exist to use our imagination to bring happiness to millions."
Walt Disney

Conclusion

Had Disney positioned his company as the one who makes cartoons for kids, the company would have disappeared several decades ago. Anyone can make cartoons for kids and for adults, but Disney built a whole empire based on this unique positioning – bringing happiness to millions of people. This is what made his company sustainable.

Intentions are fine but it is the translation of those intentions into concrete actions that can make the difference between becoming a visionary negotiator and forever remaining a wannabe.

Visionary negotiators have an ideology of future and sustainability that they share with their teams and they nurture their relationships with both external partners and their staff. Successful negotiators establish consistent alignment with their core values and goals, strategy, tactics, and practices.

Don't be anyone else doing the same thing as others. Be somebody who knows what they are doing and set the example to others. Here is how:

- Position yourself far beyond just winning. That guides and inspires the negotiating philosophy.

Winning over your competitors will only be the consequence of your sustainable negotiations.

- Be a clock-builder rather than a time-teller. Everyone can tell the time, but few people can build clocks. Time flies. Clocks stay. Time is ephemeral. Clocks are permanent.

- Don't aim at maximizing your gains – this is a short-term objective. Think about maximizing your relationships with the partners you chose. Your gains will be a natural consequence of your fruitful and sustainable cooperation.

- Stick to your core values and use the strategies that reflect them. Constancy is the way to sustainability. Use negotiators that fit in your values. They need to stand for your values and strategies.

- Sustainability implies constant progress and constant progress makes you more compelling to your potential partners and better than your competitors.

- Forget about the tyranny of *either/or* and embrace *both/and*.

- See the negotiation as a vehicle to sustainable growth and not the other way around.

- If you are well prepared, you don't need to fear getting involved in negotiations and your best reward will be to enforce the deal you signed through sustainable cooperation with your partners.

- Have clear ideas about what you want to take out of the deal you sign. And convey these ideas to your team. Don't expect people to read your mind. They might guess it wrong and their guessing can turn into certainty.

- You can benchmark other companies to see how they negotiate and which processes they implement, but keep in mind that processes can be very convenient but they are not enough. The issues can come from behaviors during the processes. Implementing new processes is useless if people don't hold one another accountable to the process. And to be accountable, you need first to understand all the interest in implementing such processes.

- More importantly, you and your team should understand that negotiation is a process and learn to behave accordingly. The international negotiation process has three main phases – before (preparation), during (encounter), and after (deal enforcement). All these phases carry the same strategic importance and are all interdependent.

- If you neglect the preparation, you will have a hard time during the negotiation rounds. If you fail your negotiation rounds, you will have a hard time enforcing the deal you signed, which is not exactly what you wanted. And if you fail in enforcing the deal, your relationship won't be sustainable and you will need to start searching for new partners over again.

Don't Be Risk-Averse

Some companies just wait and wait until they have no more options. They wait to see if luck will turn around. They wait to see what competitors do. Sometimes they don't even know what they are waiting for.

In all industries, the companies that are still around after centuries are those which didn't wait. They took the lead. They accepted or created new opportunities to themselves. And taking opportunities always entails taking risks. But they did it and they are still around. Their main competitors disappeared because they were no longer in phase with their own markets. When they realized that, it was too late.

What makes the difference is that visionary negotiators have such clarity of what they want and where they want to be in the future that they overcome all possible fears. All their focus is on getting there. They use every opportunity enabling them to leverage their progress and propel them to the position they chose for themselves.

Successful international negotiators don't see themselves just like someone working for a company and assigned with a temporary negotiation role. They see themselves as agents of progress, of evolution, and of growth. They are the best opportunities' seekers. To them, every negotiation is the opportunity of doing better, of establishing a sustainable network, and creating special opportunities to all those who collaborate with them.

Successful sustainable negotiators have been set free from the old theories and from the tyranny of dilemmas (*either/or*). They see far beyond these short-termed tactics and aim much bigger. They embrace differences and evolution and seek for what is sustainable rather than easier. Rather than fearing the unknown, they are excited by new discoveries. You can be one of them!

Bibliography

Asher, J. (2017). Close Deals Faster. Ideapress

Baker, J. (2013). 50 Quantum Physics Ideas you really need to know. Quercus.

Bhattacharjee, A., & Zhang, L. (2011). Cultural toolkit for Indians desirous of doing business in China. VIKALPA, 36(2) 59_79.

Burrough, B. & Helyar, J. (2010). Barbarians at the Gate. Arrow Books

Bynum, W. (2013). A Little Story of Science. Yale University Press

Capra, F. (1976). The Tao of physics. Bantam Books.

Cardon, P. (2009). A model of face practices in Chinese business culture: Implications for Western Businesspersons. Thunderbird International Business Review, 51(1), 19_36.

Chen, D. C. (1987). Confucius thoughts. Taipei: Cheng Chuong.

Chen, G. M., & Starosta, W. J. (1997). Chinese conflict management and resolution: Overview and implications. Intercultural Communication Studies, 7, 1_16.

Chen, M. J. (2002). Transcending paradox: The Chinese 'Middle Way' perspective. Asia Pacific Journal of Management, 19, 179_199.

Chu, S. (1974). The interpretation of I Ching. WenHua, Taipei.

Chuah, S. H., Hoffman, R., & Larner, J. (2014). Chinese values and negotiation behavior: A bargaining experiment. International Business Review, 23, 1203_1211.

Cox, B., & Forshaw, J. (2011). The Quantum Universe: Everything that can happen does happen.

Damasio, A. R. (2010). *L'Erreur de Descartes.* Odile Jacob.

Decartes, R. (1637). *Discours de la méthode pour bien conduire sa raisonet chercher la vérité dans les sciences. Les Échos du Maquis,* April 2011.

Diamond, S. (2010). Getting more. Crown Business.

Dirac, P. A. M. (1928). The quantum theory of the electron. Proceedings of the Royal Society of London. Series A, Containing Papers of a Mathematical and Physical Character,117(778), 610_624.

Eiteman, D. K. (1990). American executives' perceptions of negotiating joint ventures with the People's Republic of China: Lessons learned. Columbia Journal of World Business, 25, 59_67.

Fang, T. (1999). Chinese business negotiating style. International Business Series, Sage.

Fang, T. (2003). A critique of Hofstede's fifth national culture dimension. International Journal of Cross-Cultural Management, 3(3), 347_368.

Fang, T. (2005). From 'Onion' to 'Ocean': Paradox and change in national cultures. International Studies of Management & Organization,35, 71_90. doi: 10.1080/00208825.2005.11043743

Fang, T. (2010). Asian management research needs more self-confidence: Reflection on Hofstede (2007) and beyond. Asia Pacific Journal of Management, 27, 155_170.

Fang, T. (2011). Yin Yang: A new perspective on culture. Management and Organization Review, 5. doi: 10.1111/j.1740-8784.2011.00221.x

Fang, T. (2014). Understanding Chinese culture and communication: The Yin Yang approach. In B. Gehrke & M. C. Claes (Eds.), Global leadership practices (pp. 171_187). London: Palgrave Macmillan.

Fang, T., & Faure, G. O. (2011). Chinese communication characteristics: A Yin Yang perspective. International Journal of Intercultural Relations,35, 320_333.

Fang, T., Worm, V., & Tung, R. L. (2008). Changing success and failure factors in business negotiations with the PRC. International Business Review, 17, 159_169.

Faure, G. O. (1995). Nonverbal negotiation in China: Cycling in Beijing. Negotiation Journal, 11, 11_17.

Faure, G. O., & Fang, T. (2008). Changing Chinese values: Keeping up with paradoxes. International Business Review, (17), 194_207.

Fells, R. (2010). Effective negotiation. Cambridge: Cambridge University Press.

Fisher, R., & Shapiro, D. (1981). Beyond reason. Get what you want. Improve your relationships. Using emotions as you negotiate. Penguin.

Fisher, R., & Ury, W. (1981). Getting to yes. Houghton Mifflin Company.

Gasiorowicz, S. (1974). Quantum Physics. Wiley International Edition.

Gerry, C. C., & Knight, P. L. (1997) Quantum superpositions and Schrödinger cat states in quantum optics. American Journal of Physics,65, 964_974.

Ghauri, P., & Fang, T. (2001). Negotiating with the Chinese: A socio-cultural analysis. Journal of the World Business, 36(3), 303_325.

Gribbins, J (1984). In Search of Schrodinger's Cat. Bantam Books

Hall, E. (1976). Beyond culture. Anchor.

Heisenberg, W. (1927). *Über den anschaulichen Inhalt der quantentheoretis chen Kinematik und Mechanik*(The actual content of quantum theoretical kinematics and mechanics). Physics, 43, 172_198.

Hofstede, G. (1984). Culture's consequences. Sage.

Hofstede, G., & Hofstede, G. J. (2005). Cultures and organizations: Software of the mind. McGraw-Hill.

Johnston, P. (2007). Negotiating with Giants. Negotiation Press

Kaku, M. (1987). Beyond Einstein. Bantam Books

Kaku, M. (2008). Physics of the Impossible. Doubleday

Karsaklian, E. (2019). The After-Deal. What Happens After you Close a Deal. Information Advertising Publishing. ISBN: 9781641138079

Karsaklian, E. (2017). Sustainable Negotiation. What Physics Can Teach us About International Negotiation. Emerald Insight

Karsaklian, E. (2014). The intelligent international negotiator. Business Expert Press.

Karsaklian, E. (2016a). A Picture can be worth a thousand stories: Interpreting advertising differently in ten countries. Journal of Marketing Development and Competitiveness, 10(2).

Karsaklian, E. (2016b). The invisible negotiator in the land of paradox management. Journal of US-China Public Administration, 13(5),333_347.

Kilts, J.M. (2007). Doing what Matters. Three Rivers Press.

Leung, K. (2008). Chinese culture, modernization, and international business. International Business Review, 17, 184_187.

Leung, T. K. P., Chan, R. Y. K., Lai, K. H., & Ngai, E. W. T. (2011). An examination of the influence of guanxi and xinyong (utilization of personal trust) on negotiation outcome in China: An old-friend approach. Industrial Marketing Management, 40, 1193_1205.

Lewiki, R. J., Suanders, D. M., & Barry, B. (2011). Essentials of negotiation. McGraw-Hill International Edition.

Lewis, M. W. (2000). Exploring paradox: Toward a more comprehensive guide. Academy of Management Review, 25(4), 760_776.

Lewis, R. (2006). When cultures collide. Nicholas Brealey.

Lewis, R. (2012). When teams collide. Nicholas Brealey.

Li, P. P. (2012). Toward an integrative framework of indigenous research: The geocentric implications of Yin-Yang Balance. Asia Pacific Journal of Management, 29, 849_872.

Li, P. P. (2014). The unique value of Yin-Yang balancing: A critical response. Management and Organization Review, 10, 321_332.

Li, P. P. (2016). Global implications of the indigenous epistemological system from the east: How to apply Yin-Yang balancing to paradox management. Cross Cultural & Strategic Management, 23(1), 1_39.

Li, P. P., Leung, K., Chen, C. C., & Jar-Der Luo, J. D. (2012). Indigenous research on Chinese management: What and how. Management and Organization Review. Article first published online: March 22, 2012.doi:doi: 10.1111/j.1740-8784.2012.00292.x

Malhotra, D., & Bazerman, M. H. (2007). Negotiation Genius. Bantam Books.

McEnvoy, J. P., & Zarate, O. (1996). Quantum theory. Gutenberg Press.

McMahon, D. (2013). Quantum Mechanics Demystified. McGraw-Hill.

Merali, Z. (2015). Quantum physics: What is really real? A wave of experiments is probing the root of quantum weirdness. Accessed on July 12,2015.

Metcalf, L. E., Bird, A., Shankar Mahesh, M., Aycan, Z., Larimo, J., & Valdelamar, D. D. (2006). Cultural tendencies in negotiation: A comparison of Finland, India,

Mexico, Turkey, and the United States. Journal of World Business, 41, 382_394.

Oliver, D. (2003). How to negotiate effectively? Kogan Page.

Osman-Gani, A., & Tan, J. S. (2002). Influence of culture on negotiation styles of Asian managers: An empirical study of major cultural/ethnic groups in Singapore. Thunderbird International Business Review, 44(6),819_839.

Palich, L. E., Carini, G. R., & Livingstone, L. P. (2002). Comparing American and Chinese negotiating styles: The influence of logic paradigms. Thunderbird International Business Review, 44(6), 777_798.

Pink, D. H. (2012). To sell is human: The surprising truth about moving others. New York, NY: Riverhead.

Rae, A. I. M. (2006). Quantum physics. One World.

Rich, C. (2013). The Yes Book. Virgin Books.

Ringbauer, M., Duffus, B., Branciard, C., Cavalcanti, E. G., White, A. G. & Fedrizzi, A. (2015). Measurements of the reality of the wavefunction. Nature Physics, 11, 249_254.

Rivers, C. (2009). Negotiating with the Chinese: EANT's and all. Thunderbird International Business Review, 51(5), 473_489.

Rose, T. (2016). The End of Average. Harper One

Saee, J. (2008). Best practice in global negotiation strategies for leaders and managers in the twenty-first century. Journal of Business Economics and Management, 9(4), 309_318.

Schwartz, B. (2004). The Paradox of Choice. Why more is less. Harper Perennial.

Shi, X., & Wright, P. C. (2003). The potential impacts of national feelings on international business negotiations: a study in the China context. International Business Review, 12, 311_328.

Sparrow, G. (2014). Physics in minutes. Quercus. Stark, P. B., & Flaherty, J. (2003). The only negotiating guide you'll ever need. Broadway Books.

Stewart, S., & Keown, C. F. (1989). Talking with the dragon: Negotiating in the People's Republic of China. Columbia Journal of World Business,24, 68_72.

Tian, X. (2007). Managing international business in China. Cambridge: Cambridge University Press.

Tihanyi, L., Griffith, D. A., & Russell, C. J. (2005). The effect of cultural distance on entry mode choice, international diversification, and MNE performance: a meta-analysis. Journal of International Business Studies,36, 270_283.

Trompenaars, F., & Hampden-Turner, C. (2006). Riding the waves of culture. Nicholas Brealey.

Ury, W. (1991). Getting past NO. Bantam Books.

Ury, W. (2008). The power of positive NO. Hodder & Stoughton. Waldman, G. (2002). Introduction to light: The physics of light, vision, and color. Dover Publications.

Walsh, J. P., Wang, E., & Xin, K. R. (1999). Same bed, different dreams: Working relationships in Sino-American joint ventures. Journal of the World Business, 34(1), 69_93.

Yau, O. (1988). Chinese cultural values: Their dimensions and marketing implications. European Journal of Marketing, 22(5), 44_57.

Zhang, H., & Baker, G. (2008). Think like Chinese. The Federation Press